The Atlas of
Natural
Disasters

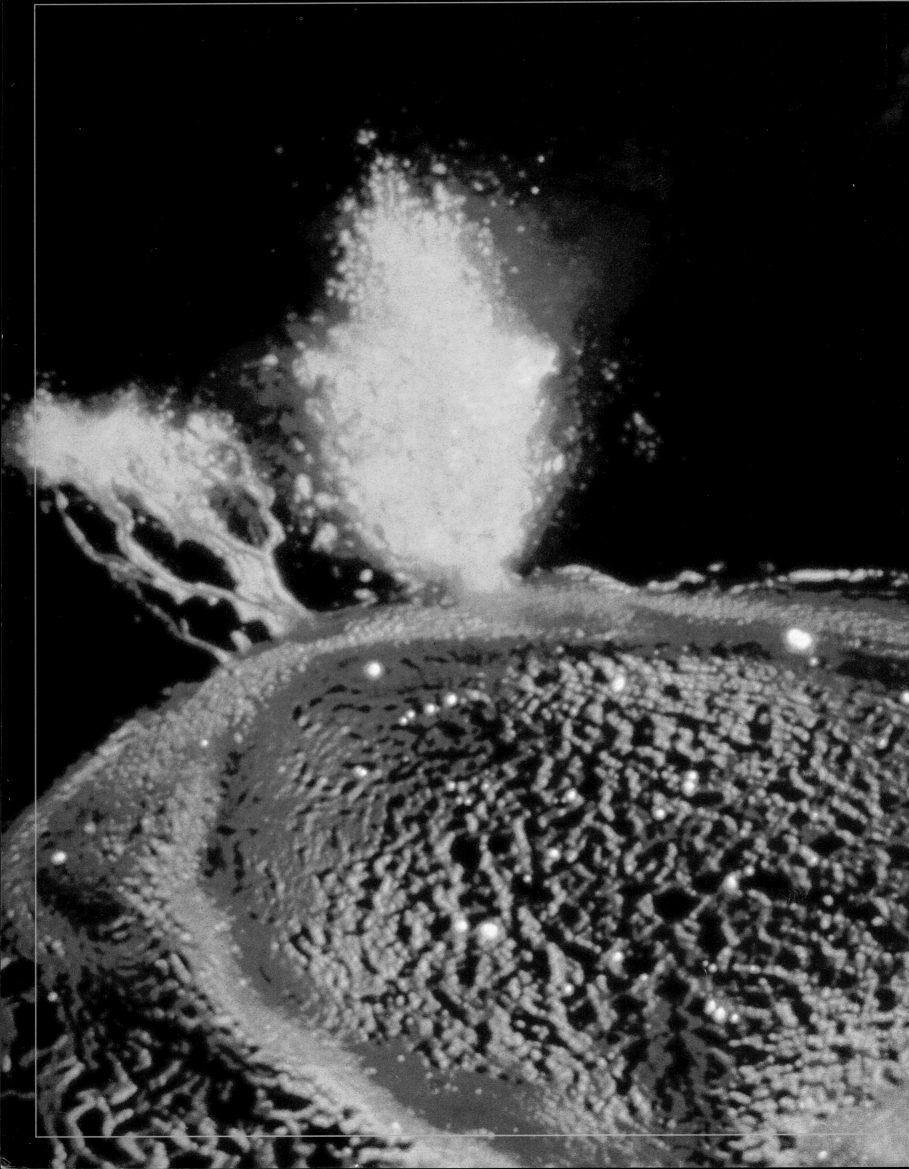

The Atlas of
Natural
Disasters

JEFF GROMAN

THE ATLAS OF NATURAL DISASTERS

Z-Publishing Ltd.
7-11 St. Johns Hill
London SW11 1TN
United Kingdom

This edition published in North America
2002 by Michael Friedman Publishing Group, Inc.
Originally published by Z-Publishing Ltd. © 2001

ISBN 1-4027-0323-6
10 9 8 7 6 5 4 3 2 1

Created and produced by
Fire Publishing Limited
1 Torriano Mews, London NW5 2RZ

Project Director
Nicholas Bevan

Editor
Quentin Daniel

Art Editor
Bob Burroughs

Picture Research
Mirco Decet, Vanessa Fletcher
Fact Checker
Cathy Johns
Proofreader
Neil Morris
Indexer
Marie Lorimer

Illustrations by
Julian Baker, Colin Woodman

Printed in China

Contents

 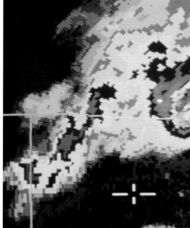  

A Turbulent Planet

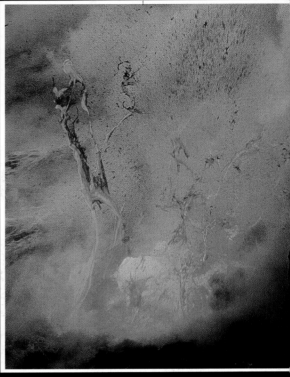

Lava spews out of an Icelandic volcano.

FOR AT LEAST 4,000 MILLION YEARS, the Earth has been in motion, spinning on its own axis once every 24 hours at a speed of 66,614 miles per hour (107,200 kmh) and completing one orbit of the Sun roughly once a year. But the planet's surface is also on the move. Made up of segments known as tectonic plates, the Earth's crust is constantly shifting above a layer of molten rock. Over hundreds of millions of years, such movements have positioned and formed the oceans and continents.

Of course, the forces released by the motions of the Earth's crust are simply colossal. The molten rock beneath the crust sometimes seeks escape, and volcanic eruptions are the result. These have had, and continue to have, their own catastrophic effects on the planet's surface

Searching for earthquake survivors in Turkey.

A hurricane forming off the coast of Florida.

and the life on it, as have earthquakes triggered by the grinding and shearing of tectonic plates.

But it is not simply the ground beneath our feet that is unpredictable. Clouds form all the time in the Earth's atmosphere and drop rain and snow over land and sea. While such moisture is necessary for the continuation of life itself, too much can have a lethal effect. In the past 100 years alone, floods brought about by storms of all kinds have killed millions of people worldwide. On the other hand, lack of rain can also have terrible consequences, as the African droughts of the 20th century have proved.

And nature besieges human beings on yet a third front. Earth is, first and foremost, a watery planet. The oceans cover about 70 percent of the surface and currents run like huge rivers through them. Waves

A tornado whirls through the American Midwest.

A dried-out riverbed in Namibia, Africa.

caused by winds, tides, or even earthquakes batter shorelines and change their shape, while rivers making their way to the sea constantly remold the land. Sea and river floods frequently destroy entire communities. The lives of millions of people round the world involve a constant struggle to keep such floodwaters at bay.

Terrible as these violent motions of earth, air, and water are to their victims, on the whole they must be seen as the natural lot of all living creatures on Earth. And since their appearance on Earth about 500,000 years ago, humans have had a hard enough task to survive them. But the last 200 years have witnessed a further, more disturbing development: humans are

Forest fires rage in California.

An oil slick in the Persian Gulf.

themselves having a destructive effect on the environment. The air we breathe is being poisoned by chemicals, as are the rivers and seas. Rain forests are being destroyed, the last wildernesses are threatened with development, and there are deserts where there were once seas or lakes. Many animal and plant species are becoming extinct, and the world's human population is spiraling out of control....

The stubborn endurance of the human race in the face of such natural terrors as earthquakes and storms may sometimes seem nothing short of miraculous. But a still greater miracle would be if we were to halt the harm we ourselves are now doing to the planet.

Crowds in the streets of Dhaka, Bangladesh.

The Shifting Surface

T HE EARTH'S CRUST is a layer of rock encasing the planet. Varying between 5 miles (8 km) thick under the oceans to about 25 miles (40 km) thick under the continents, the crust is not one solid piece but made up of 30 separate plates. These shift about on the mantle, a thick layer of red-hot molten rock, at a rate of up to 4 inches (10 cm) a year. Cracks called faults appear in the Earth's crust, allowing molten rock from the mantle to escape upward through vents. Volcanic eruptions are often the result.

But along some faults, the rocks are fixed, unable to slide as the plates move. The pressure builds up, the rocks shatter, and huge tremors travel through the Earth—earthquakes. Both volcanoes and earthquakes have a huge impact on the Earth's surface and the life on it.

Volcanoes: The Fire-breathers

Volcanoes fall into three main categories, according to the shape of their cones. "Cinder cones" (such as Hawaiian Pu'u O'o, above) form when rock fragments erupt from a vent and fall back to earth to build up a cone shape. "Shield" volcanoes, on the other hand, are created when free-flowing lava spreads widely over the surrounding landscape to form a low, dome-shaped mountain. A number of other volcanoes in Hawaii are shield volcanoes. "Composite" volcanoes, lastly, are created when lava and rock fragments erupt to form a towering mountain. Mount Vesuvius in Italy is a composite volcano, as is Mount St. Helens in the northwestern U.S.

BELOW: *November 1973—molten lava from the Hawaiian volcano of Kilauea cascades into a lava lake some 495 feet (151 m) across.*

A VOLCANIC ERUPTION is one of the most awe-inspiring of all natural events. The power an eruption unleashes can be devastating, and volcanic activity tends to have a lasting effect on the surrounding landscape and its inhabitants.

Volcanoes are essentially openings in the Earth's surface where molten rock or magma beneath the planet's crust rises up and seeks escape. Leaving the central "vent" and flowing down the volcano's slopes, the magma—now called "lava"—can lay waste forests or farmland and may threaten or engulf nearby villages. As they cool and harden, lava flows may add yet another layer of matter to the cone shape of many volcanoes.

Yet lava is not the only material spewed out by an eruption. Clouds of steam and dust billow out, while mudflows of ash and water may slide down the volcano's slopes. Ash may also coat the land for many miles.

Devastation caused by fire and ash.

Lava flows, which will cool and harden to form stratified layers of volcanic rock.

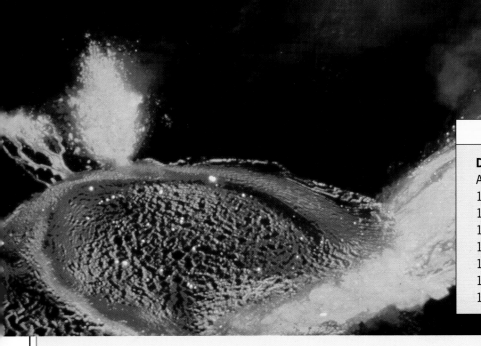

FAMOUS ERUPTIONS

Date	Place	Death toll
AD 79	Vesuvius, Italy	20,000
1669	Mount Etna, Italy	20,000
1815	Mount Tambora, Indonesia	92,000
1883	Krakatoa, Indonesia	36,000
1902	Mont Pelée, Martinique	30,000
1919	Kelud, Indonesia	5500
1985	Nevado del Ruiz, Colombia	22,000
1991	Mt. Pinatubo, Philippines	1000

See also:
• **Volcanic Eruptions: The Danger Signs** *p. 14–15*
• **Mount St. Helens: A Giant Awakes** *p. 16–17*

Main areas of
volcanic activity

Volcanic "bombs."
Such "bombs"
range from football-
sized rock frag-
ments to monstrous
boulders weighing
up to 90 tons (82
metric tons).

BELOW: *A composite
illustration of various
kinds of volcanic
activity. When a
volcanic "bomb" is
blasted out by an
eruption, it is usually
a sign of blockage in
the volcano's vent.*

LEFT: *On the
Hawaiian volcano
Kalapana, lava tubes
(within which molten lava
flows) collapse, exposing
the lava beneath. Tubes
keep the lava fluid and
scorching hot.*

Erratic bursts
of ash and
hot lava.

The volcanic vent,
which pipes the
magma up to the
volcano's mouth.

The magma
chamber
under the
Earth's
crust.

KILLERS AND CREATORS

The destructive force of molten
lava flowing down a volcano's
side can be enormous. It has been
estimated that in the last 600 years
more than 200,000 people have been
killed worldwide by volcanic activity.
Volcanic activity occurs mainly in
places where the rigid plates that
make up the Earth's outer shell meet
and are in motion. These
areas include the so-
called "Ring of Fire"
that encircles Iceland
(right), Hawaii, and
southern Europe.

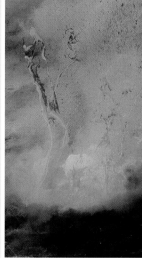

Life-giving ash
Yet whether volcanoes
are described as "active"
(erupting constantly),
"intermittent" (erupting
at regular intervals),
"dormant" (inactive but
not dead), or "extinct"
(inactive in historical
times), many people still
live in close proximity to
them. This is because volcanic ash
produces a rich soil on nearby
plains, and valuable chemical
deposits are found in volcanic materials, including sulphur and mercury.
Lava rock is also used for road
building. In many volcanic regions
throughout the world, such as New
Zealand, the U.S., Italy, Mexico, and
Iceland, underground steam is used
as a source of energy to
produce electricity and heating.

RIGHT: *A lava flow cool-
ing on the slopes of a
volcano. The shapes lava
flows take depend on the
thickness and movement
of the lava itself.*

Volcanic Eruptions: The Danger Signs

ASH CLOUDS

Volcanic ash and other debris thrown into the atmosphere can affect the world's climate. Below are some famous eruptions and the approximate amount of airborne debris they created above the Earth.

● Mt. Tambora, Indonesia (1815): 12 square miles
● Mt. Krakatoa, Indonesia (1883): 8 square miles
● Mt. Katmai, Alaska (1912): 5.2 square miles
● Mt. Pinatubo, Philippines (1991): 3.2 square miles
● Mt. Vesuvius, Italy (AD 79): 2 square miles
● Mt. Fuji, Japan (1707): 1.6 square miles

LAVA FIREWORKS

The volcano on the island of Stromboli, which lies in the Tyrrhenian Sea off the southern Italian coast, is one of the few in Europe that is constantly active. It is 3048 feet (929 m) high and its spectacular eruptions include "lava fountains" and partially molten volcanic "bombs" (below).

Fortunately, since the lava flows freely down the slopes of Stromboli's volcano instead of building up pressure inside it, the eruptions are limited in size and rarely pose a threat to the island's population.

THERE ARE several telltale signs that mean a volcano is about to erupt. Magma forcing its way to the surface causes the earth to shake, and the best way to measure the force and frequency of these tremors is with an instrument called a seismometer. If the seismometer registers an increase in earth tremors, it may mean that an eruption will happen soon.

A tiltmeter is another useful tool in the prediction of eruptions. This instrument indicates whether a volcano is swelling—a sure sign that magma is rising inside it. Also, the temperature of lakes and hot springs near a volcano will often rise before an eruption, and gases will be given off via various vents in the mountainside. Sensitive thermometers and gas detectors help scientists to monitor such activity.

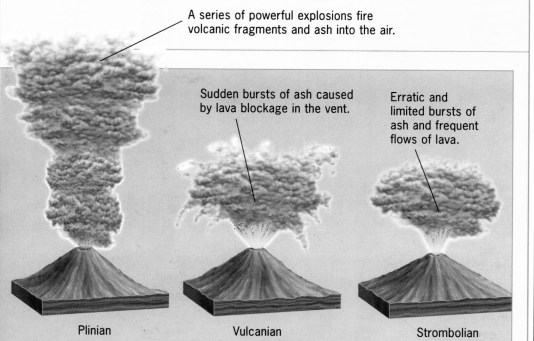

A series of powerful explosions fire
volcanic fragments and ash into the air.

Sudden bursts of ash caused
by lava blockage in the vent.

Erratic and
limited bursts of
ash and frequent
flows of lava.

Plinian   Vulcanian   Strombolian

ABOVE: *Three kinds of eruptions. As well as the various shapes of
volcanic cone, eruptions help scientists to classify volcanoes. Other
kinds of eruptions are "Hawaiian" (where lava flows constantly) and
"Pelean" (where ash and gas cover the mountain slopes).*

ABOVE: *Alaska's Augustine volcano in mid-eruption.
Augustine produced a series of pyroclastic flows—
fast-moving avalanches of hot lava fragments and
billowing ash that caused extensive damage to the
surrounding landscape.*

ABOVE: *Darkness descends on Plymouth,
the capital of Montserrat (a small
Caribbean island), as an ash cloud from a
volcanic eruption blots out the Sun.*

REDUCING DESTRUCTION

No human power can stop
a volcano from erupting.
Even so, scientists are learning
more about volcanic eruptions
and their effects so that they
can save lives and minimize
damage in the future.

Poisonous gases
Many poisonous gases con-
tained in magma are released
into both the atmosphere and
the earth during an eruption.
The dead and dying trees on
the side of Mammoth
Mountain volcano in eastern
California (below) were caused
by carbon dioxide gas in
magma flowing under the
mountain, while volcanic

clouds in Hawaii (above) contain deadly sulphur dioxide
that can suffocate living creatures and destroy vegetation.
Landslides and the silting-up of
riverbeds are added dangers.

From slow to fast
Lava flows usually move slowly
enough for people to avoid
them, and sometimes it is possible for the flow to be
diverted or stopped. But
if the lava flow consists
of a mixture of hot, dry
rock fragments and hot
gases spewing from a vent
at high speed, then there
may be little choice but to
evacuate the area.

Mount St. Helens: A Giant Awakes

5:56 Plumes of steam herald the moment of eruption.

6:25 Eruptive lava and other debris flow down the mountainside.

6:27 Massive clouds of ash begin to billow out of the crater.

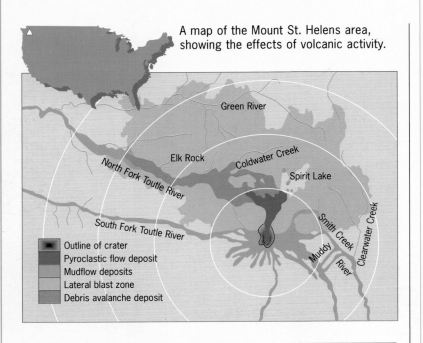

A map of the Mount St. Helens area, showing the effects of volcanic activity.

Green River

Elk Rock   Coldwater Creek

North Fork Toutle River

Spirit Lake

South Fork Toutle River

Smith Creek

Clearwater Creek

Muddy River

- Outline of crater
- Pyroclastic flow deposit
- Mudflow deposits
- Lateral blast zone
- Debris avalanche deposit

MONITORING THE MOUNTAIN

Scientists studying Mount St. Helens in the 1970s had predicted an eruption before the year 2000. By March 1980, the signs of danger were growing as thousands of small tremors shook the mountain. Two months later their worst fears were realized.

Eruption prediction
The U.S. Geological Survey (below) has since set up continuous and highly detailed monitoring programs on the mountain to predict the size of any future eruption. Their activities include building instrument stations near the dome, measuring cracks in the crater floor, collecting and analyzing gas samples, and measuring changes in the magnetic field.

On the morning of May 18, 1980, people living near the Cascade Mountains in Washington State, U.S., felt the ground shudder beneath them. It was a magnitude 5.1 earthquake that soon passed away – but not before it had caused a massive landslide on a nearby volcano.

Though Mount St. Helens had erupted many times over the past 5,000 years, for 123 years it had remained dormant. Now the earthquake and landslide released the enormous pressures that had built up inside it, and an enormous eruption followed.

The initial blast hurled the top off the volcano, creating a large crater and reducing its height from 9,850 to 8,530 feet (3,000 to 2,600 m). Billowing out after it to a height of 15 miles (25 km) came an ash cloud made of magma and steam. This cloud drifted in an easterly direction to deposit ash as far as Wisconsin, 2,000 miles (3,000 km) away. Rock fragments were also spewed up and rained down over an area that extended some 30 miles (50 km) from the volcano itself.

By early morning the next day, the eruption was over—but at the tragic cost of 60 lives.

ABOVE: *A plume of steam rising 3,250 feet (1,000 m) above the rim of the Mount St. Helens crater. This photo was taken two years after the first big eruption.*

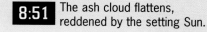

6:43 Ash clouds form a pillar rising many miles into the air.

7:10 Volcanic material continues to spew from the crater.

8:51 The ash cloud flattens, reddened by the setting Sun.

ABOVE: *The eruption as it happened. The landslide's unblocking of the volcano's vent produced a blast that hurled nearly 27,000 cubic feet (764 cubic m) of material across the landscape. A crater was formed, and pyroclastic flows poured out of it down the north flank into the valley below. Meanwhile, a huge ash cloud spread out in an easterly direction.*

DEVASTATION AND RENEWAL

The May 1980 eruption of Mount St. Helens caused huge damage over an area covering 40 square miles (100 sq km). All man-made structures around nearby Spirit Lake were damaged or buried under ash and mud. More than 200 miles (300 km) of roads and 15 miles (25 km) of railway tracks and bridges were completely obliterated by floods, mudslides and volcanic debris, while mudflows dumped millions of tonnes of sediment into rivers, valleys, and reservoirs.

ABOVE: *Felled trees lie scattered like matchsticks on the slopes, victims of volcanic mudflows.*

Forests destroyed
But it was the region's forests that suffered most. Many tens of thousands of acres (hectares), which included millions of tons of usable timber (enough to build 150,000 homes), were lost. Forest

BELOW: *Nature's resilience – a flush of vegetation reappears on the ash-covered slopes.*

wildlife also suffered heavily. While many small animals such as mice, frogs, and gophers were hibernating below ground or underwater and were able to survive, larger animals such as bears, deer, and coyotes perished in vast numbers. But as vegetation started to reappear, these bigger animals began to make their way back from surrounding areas.

GROWTH OF A DOME
Inside the crater formed by the explosion of Mount St. Helens in May 1980, a lava dome has steadily been growing:
● In 1980 it was 112 feet (34 m) high and over 1,000 feet (300 m) wide.
● In 1981 it was 535 feet (163 m) and 1,310 feet (0.4 km) wide.
● In 1995 it was 1,150 feet (230 m) high and 3,445 feet (0.8 km) wide.
● By 2180——should growth continue at the present rate——the mountain should have regained its pre-1980 size.

Earthquakes: The Shaking Crust

EARTHQUAKE ZONES

Most earthquakes occur along the edges of the world's tectonic plates, the segments that make up the Earth's crust (below, with orange showing the main quake zones). When the plates grind against each other, they cause an explosion of energy underground. Two plates meet along the western coast of North America. Others meet along the western rim of the Pacific and along the edge of North Africa.

But quakes can also occur far from plate edges. In 1811, three quakes occurred in Missouri, in the middle of North America, while in 1990 a magnitude 5.2 quake struck Great Britain.

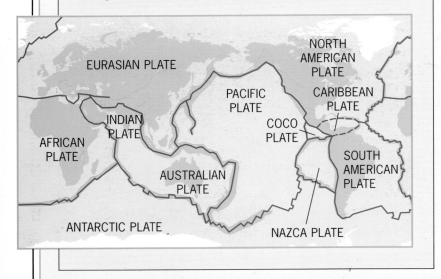

A POWERFUL EARTHQUAKE can release more destructive energy than the combined explosive force of 10,000 atomic bombs. Fortunately, such quakes occur only about once every two years worldwide. Still, every year about 40 are violent enough to cause limited damage, while some 50,000 small quakes or tremors are registered on sensitive recorders known as seismometers.

Earthquakes usually begin underground when the large sections that make up the Earth's crust – the tectonic plates – grind against each other and shift into new positions. The energy released spreads rapidly through the ground in the form of vibrations. The place where rock first shatters is called the quake's focus, and the point on the surface directly above it is known as its epicenter. This is where damage to the Earth's surface – and everything on it – is most severe.

LEFT: *The aftermath of the 1995 quake in Kobe, Japan. Hit by tremors, buildings collapsed to crush or bury alive many of the quake's 5,000 victims.*

GREAT QUAKES

Date	Location	Magnitude*	Death Toll
1201	Northern Egypt	Unknown	1.1 million
1556	Central China	Unknown	830,000
1737	Calcutta, India	Unknown	300,000
1908	Messina, Sicily	7.5	120,000
1920	Gansu, China	8.6	200,000
1927	Nan-shan, China	8.3	200,000
1948	Turkmenistan	7.3	100,000
1970	Peru	7.7	66,000
1976	Tangshan, China	8.1	240,000
1978	Northeast Iran	7.7	25,000
1988	Armenia	7.0	25,000
1990	Northwest Iran	7.5	40,000
1993	Southern India	6.4	10,000
1995	Kobe, Japan	7.2	5,000

*(Richter scale)

See also:
- **The San Andreas Fault: Brink of Disaster** *p. 20–21*
- **Tsunamis: Waves of Terror** *p. 58–59*

Main areas of
earthquake activity...

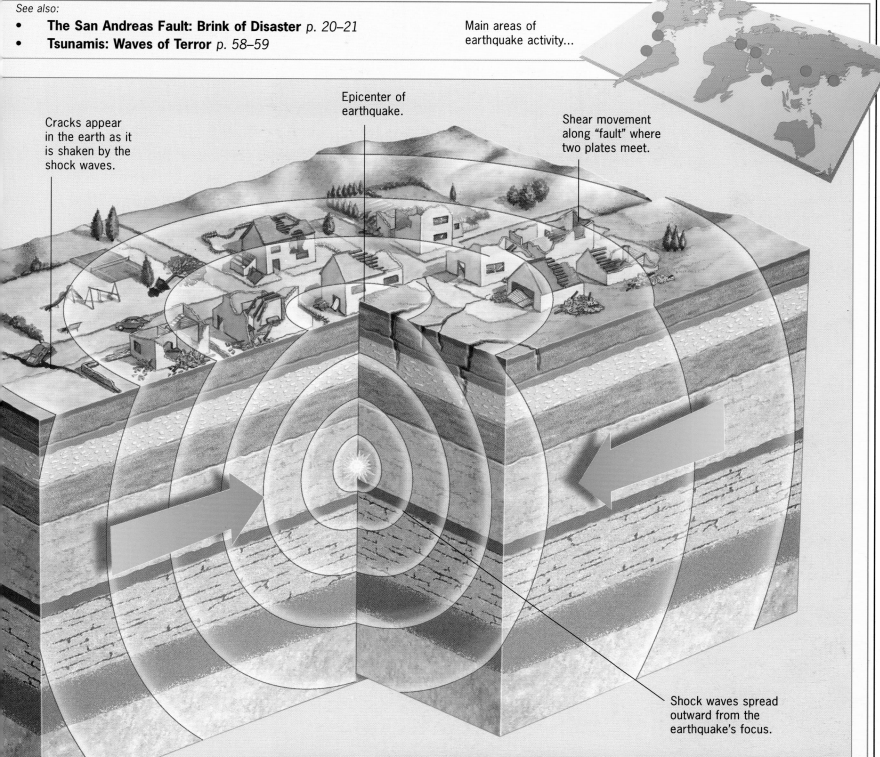

Cracks appear
in the earth as it
is shaken by the
shock waves.

Epicenter of
earthquake.

Shear movement
along "fault" where
two plates meet.

Shock waves spread
outward from the
earthquake's focus.

ABOVE: *Anatomy of an earth-quake, showing how the move-ment along the edges of two tectonic plates exerts enormous pressure on rock strata under-ground. Shock waves then spread from the earthquake's focus, to hit the surface hardest directly above. In the 1995 quake in Kobe, Japan, the oldest buildings – those without any steel reinforcement – were the first to collapse (right).*

The San Andreas Fault: Brink of Disaster

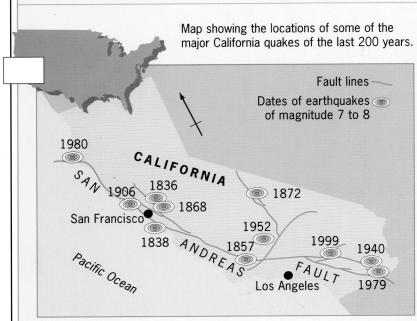

Map showing the locations of some of the major California quakes of the last 200 years.

Fault lines

Dates of earthquakes of magnitude 7 to 8

CALIFORNIA

SAN

1980

1906 1836 1868

1872

San Francisco

ANDREAS

1952

1838 1857

1999 1940

Pacific Ocean

FAULT

Los Angeles 1979

BELOW: *An illustration of the San Andreas Fault, showing shear movement along it north and south. Extending from a position just off the coast of northwest California to the southeast part of the state, the fault has many adjacent faults. The entire system is 79.5 miles (1,280 km) long and up to 652 miles (1,050 km) wide.*

I N 1906, A SEVERE EARTHQUAKE struck San Francisco, California, and caused one of the worst disasters in American history. more than 700 people died and some 28,000 buildings were destroyed. The cause of the quake was shear movement along the San Andreas Fault—the great scarlike fissure where the Pacific tectonic plate meets the North American Plate.

Moving between 1 to 1.5 inches (2.5 to 3.7 cm) every year, the fault is responsible for frequent earth tremors. Most do little damage, but occasionally there is major seismic activity. In 1989, for example, a 32-foot (10 m) section of the Bay Bridge from Oakland to San Francisco collapsed due to earth tremors, and 62 people died. Scientists are even now wondering when the so-called Big One will hit California.

ABOVE: *San Francisco after the quake of April 18, 1906. It struck at 5:13 A.M., when most people were sleeping.*

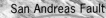

San Francisco

The edge of the Pacific Plate slides northward, taking western California with it.

San Andreas Fault

North American Plate

Los Angeles

Pacific Plate

The edge of the North American Plate slides southward, grinding against the Pacific Plate.

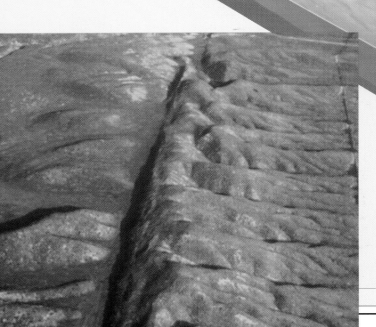

LEFT: *The San Andreas Fault at its most visible and dramatic—splitting the Carrizo Plain 99 miles (160 km) north of Los Angeles.*

SAN ANDREAS QUAKES

Date	Location	Magnitude*
1812	Santa Barbara Channel	7.0
1857	Fort Tejon	8.5
1868	Hayward Fault	7.0
1906	San Francisco	8.5
1922	Eureka	7.3
1940	Imperial Valley	7.1
1971	San Fernando	6.1
1979	Imperial Valley	6.5
1980	Eureka	7.2
1987	Superstition Hills	6.6
1989	Loma Prieta	7.1

*Richter scale

ABOVE AND RIGHT: *The legacy of a powerful California quake— buckled highways, twisted girders, and many casualties. Luckily, most quake activity in the region does not amount to more than minor tremors.*

Izmit, 1999: A Turkish Tragedy

TURKISH QUAKES

● It is thought that more than 25,000 people perished in an earthquake in Antioch (modern Antakya) in A.D. 526.

● Over the past 75 years, more than 20 Turkish quakes have exceeded 6.0 on the Richter scale.

● In 1939 a quake in Erzincan in the east of the country killed more than 30,000 people.

● In 1998 a quake in the city of Adana killed 144 people and injured more than 1,500.

● A 1997 study estimated a 12 percent chance of a quake hitting Izmit before 2020.

ABOVE AND BELOW:
Rescue operations in Izmit—a race against time with air running out for survivors trapped under rubble, and with the possibility of after-shocks ever present in the rescuers' minds.

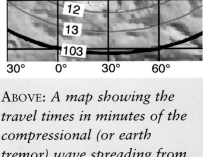

ABOVE: *A map showing the travel times in minutes of the compressional (or earth tremor) wave spreading from the Izmit quake to points around the globe.*

I N THE EARLY HOURS of the morning on August 17, 1999, most people in the Turkish city of Izmit were asleep in their beds. Then, at 3:01, an earthquake originating at a depth of 11 miles (17 km) and with its epicenter about 7 miles (11 km), from Izmit hit the surface and the whole town shook. Within seconds buildings began to collapse, killing thousands of people as they slept and leaving tens of thousands homeless.

The earthquake measured 7.4 on the Richter scale and produced up to 37 miles (60 km) of cracks in the Earth's surface. The damage was particularly intense because the source of the quake was shallow. This meant that shock waves could not even be partially absorbed by rock strata and soil before they hit the surface.

AVERTING DISASTER

As Turkish rescue teams worked around the clock to try to reach victims trapped in the rubble, public anger grew as to why so many buildings were not able to withstand the effects of the quake. This was despite the fact that scientists, using seismological technology (see below), had been predicting such a disaster in the region for many years. With over 1,000 rural migrants flowing into Izmit and Istanbul every day, it is believed cheaply built illegal housing was mainly responsible for the high death toll. Older buildings made of solid material withstood the quake, while modern mud-brick structures folded like card houses. To avert such disasters in the future, it will be necessary both to heed scientists' warnings and build shock-absorbent structures.

Satellite relaying data.

Sensor in water well monitors groundwater level.

Surface deformation recorder.

Creepometer records surface movement.

Seismometer measures force of shock.

Laser beams bounced against reflectors measure surface movement.

Reflector

Magnometer records shifts in magnetic field.

ABOVE AND BELOW: *Collapsed buildings in Izmit—as much the result of poor construction as the force of the quake. A total of 65 percent of all buildings in Turkey are constructed without an official permit.*

Landslides: The Force of Gravity

ABOVE: *When the solid rock under a slope is weakened, the topsoil will often break away in slabs, causing landslides. Slippage (below) can threaten houses from underneath as well.*

LANDSLIDES ARE DANGEROUS masses of rock and earth that slither down steep mountain slopes. Though they are usually caused by earthquakes or torrential rain, they can also be triggered by heavy traffic and construction projects such as road building.

The most landslide-prone areas tend to be deforested or glacier-eroded mountainsides. In Italy alone, 1,000 towns and villages are at risk today from falling rocks, while in Los Angeles, homes are constantly being destroyed by debris falling from nearby hills. But one of the most frightening landslides of all took place in China in 1985. A huge chunk of cliff face toppled into the Yangtze River, and the wave it created was over 120 feet (36 m) high.

RIGHT: *One method of stopping houses from being swept away by smaller landslides is to build them on "jacks" or small hydraulic stilts.*

See also:
- **Mudslides: Moving Quagmires** *p. 28–29*
- **Avalanches: The White Menace** *p. 30–31*

CONTROLLING LANDSLIDES

Landslides are difficult to control. But checks such as drainage systems and concrete buttresses, as well as the use of steel bolts to hold cliff faces together, can do much to prevent landslides in the first place.

In Japan in 1938, almost 130,000 houses were destroyed and 500 people killed by landslides. By 1976, the country's worst year for landslides in 20 years, measures had brought the numbers down to 2,000 homes destroyed and just over 100 people killed.

ABOVE: *A landslide caused by the collapse of an irrigation system. The continual grinding action of waves on cliffs (left) or lake shorelines (far left) can also cause severe landslides.*

MAJOR LANDSLIDES

Year	Place	Cause	Death Toll
1881	Elm, Switzerland	Quarrying	115
1920	Gansu, China	Earthquake	200,000
1962	Huascaran, Peru	Earthquake	4,000
1974	Mayunmarca, Peru	Earthquake	200

After a Landslide: Picking up the Pieces

A little girl carries a bucketful of precious water after a landslide.

Rescue workers search debris for both the living and the dead.

A makeshift ambulance speeds away with one of the injured.

ABOVE: *Attempting to get past a landslide covering part of a mountain road in northern Pakistan.*

LANDSLIDES CAN BURY whole communities under rock and earth or else simply sweep them away. Roads and bridges can be destroyed or made impassable, the streets of towns may be strewn with wreckage and debris, and there may be torrential rain or earthquake aftershocks to contend with.

Such appalling conditions make the task of rescue workers and aid organizations all the more difficult—yet they must work fast if they are to save the lives of those who have survived the initial catastrophe. Survivors, who are often in a state of deep shock, must be given medical aid, shelter, food, and water. And there is a still grimmer task to perform: The dead must be dug out of the rubble to prevent the spread of disease.

But this is only the beginning. It may take many years and millions of dollars to reconstruct landslide-hit regions.

LEFT: *A landslide-shattered road in the Philippines. The sheer force of material sliding down a mountainside causes such upheaval.*

Survivors clamber past a car crushed by concrete and corrugated roofs.

Rescuers haul on a cable to drag away debris.

Shocked survivors survey the wreckage of their town.

ABOVE: *Soldiers and sniffer dogs scour a hillside for signs of life beneath the rubble.*

Mudslides: Moving Quagmires

ABOVE: *This mudslide in a partially deforested area of California was caused by heavy rain. A mountain cabin had a lucky escape.*

UNNATURAL CAUSES

Both landslides and mudslides can be triggered by human activity. When forests are cleared on mountain slopes or extensive quarrying takes place, torrential rain can turn these areas into a sea of fast-moving mud (below). This is exactly what happened when a cyclone struck the Philippine islands of Leyte and Negros in 1991. Vast areas of deforested mountainside came loose and descended on towns and villages to kill thousands of people.

ON MAY 31, 1970, an earthquake rocked a 22,205 feet (6,768 m) high peak in the Andes mountains of Peru, South America, about 199 miles (320 km) from the country's capital, Lima. On the lower slopes of the mountain, 360 million square feet (100 million cubic m) of earth and rock came loose and hurtled down a cliff face. Combining with glacier and river waters, this landslide became a muddy wave over 200 feet (62 m) high, which competely obliterated every town and village in its path for over 50 miles (80 km). More than 20,000 people lost their lives.

Although this South American disaster was on an almost unimaginable scale, mudslides do occur quite frequently in many parts of the world. Essentially a form of landslide combined with mud from mountain slopes, they are often started by earthquakes—though they can be caused by torrential rain alone.

See also:
- **Landslides: The Force of Gravity** p. 24–25
- **Avalanches: The White Menace** p. 30–31

ABOVE: *A diagram of a mudslide in mid-flow. The tonguelike shape of the mudslide is typical. Obviously, the steeper the slope, the greater the momentum of the slide as it moves downhill.*

RIGHT: *The aftermath of a mudslide in Sikkim, northeastern India—a product of deforestation. Houses stand little chance against the sheer weight of mudslides (below).*

ANTI-MUD MEASURES

Once a tide of mud is flowing rapidly down a mountain slope, nothing can stop it. Nonetheless, some measures can be taken to lessen the chances of a mudslide occurring.

Tarpaulin protection

On some exposed slopes, for example, vast tarpaulins can be laid down (below) to protect the earth from heavy rain. Mats pinned to the mountainside perform very much the same function. But reducing deforestation and the construction of adequate drainage systems are the only truly effective ways of avoiding mudslides.

Avalanches: The White Menace

BELOW: *As a huge slab avalanche moves down a mountain slope, it breaks into pieces.*
BELOW RIGHT: *A dry avalanche develops a cloudlike "swirl" as it goes downhill.*

Slab avalanche

Dry avalanche

IMAGINE YOU ARE STANDING on a snowbound mountainside, resting after a long ski down. Suddenly you hear a rumbling roar from the mountaintop, and look up to see a huge white cloud descending toward you at increasing speed. . . . This is an avalanche, a mass of snow loosened from the mountainside by heavy winds or rain, by earth tremors, or even by loud noises and skiers. There are three main kinds of avalanches. A "dry" avalanche is powdery, crisp snow that speeds down a mountain at up to 186 miles per hour (300 kmh). A "slab" avalanche is a solid portion of snow—often over 330 feet (100 m) wide and 33 feet (10 m) thick—that breaks loose and splits into pieces as it descends. And a "wet" avalanche is a slithering mass of dense, slushy snow.

ABOVE: *A dry avalanche tumbles down a mountainside. Such dense, powdery flurries move with extraordinary speed and can envelop the fastest skier.*

AVALANCHE DISASTERS

Date	Place	Death toll
1910	Washington State	120
1950–54	Switzerland and Austria	400
1962	Peru	4,000
1971	Peru	500
1979	India	200

(During World War I, many thousands were killed in the Italian Alps by avalanches caused by combat activity.)

See also:
- **Landslides: The Force of Gravity** *p. 24–25*
- **Mudslides: Moving Quagmires** *p. 28–29*

Main areas of
avalanche activity

ENTOMBED BY SNOW

The chances of surviving an avalanche are slim. Caught in a torrent of snow, ice, and rocks, many victims are hurled over and over and eventually come to rest upside down, trapped in a tomb of ice in which they soon die from cold and lack of air. Only about five percent of avalanche casualties are rescued alive.

Rescuers search for survivors by probing the snow with long poles called sounding rods and

using specialized equipment that can detect metallic objects, such as skis, and body warmth. Dogs, such as St. Bernards and German shepherds (see below left), are also employed.

Anti-avalanche measures
The destructive force and frequency of avalanches can be controlled to some extent. In avalanche areas, houses are often built with extra-strong foundations, while huge rock walls can be built above villages. Explosives can be set off to avoid excessive snow buildup and trees replanted on affected slopes. Snow slopes can also be stabilized by fences. Avoiding dangerous mountain slopes is yet another obvious safety measure, as is expert scrutiny of avalanche conditions and warnings issued to local people and holiday skiers alike.

BELOW: *While forests are often the first to suffer from avalanches, they are essential to slow their progress and maintain firm snow conditions on the mountain.*

BELOW: *Snow fences work in two ways to prevent avalanches: They hinder snow buildup and they slow down a mass of snow once it has begun to slither downhill.*

LEFT: *Climbers make their way up a snowbound mountainside in Pakistan, keeping one eye on the progress of a small "dry" avalanche on nearby Hilden Peak.*

South Carolina

Georgia

Florida

The Bahamas

CUBA

The Restless Atmosphere

W EATHER AND CLIMATE affect all life on Earth, determining the lushness of vegetation, the health of crops and—vitally—the extent of water supplies. But weather should not be confused with climate, which is the average temperature of a large region and the amount of rain it receives over a long period.

On the other hand, nearly all weather conditions occur over short periods and are more or less local in effect. They develop in the lowest part of the atmosphere and are constantly changing. Severe weather can include lightning-laden thunderstorms, hurricanes that swirl destructively over equatorial regions, and tornadoes created by the collision of warm and cool air.

Hurricanes: Storm Force

ABOVE: *Coastal palm trees lashed by the wind during a hurricane. Hurricane damage is mainly confined to coasts and islands. As the storm moves inland, it begins to lose the energy it derived from warm seawater.*

TRACKING HURRICANES

In a hurricane, winds rotate around a calm area at the center of the storm known as the "eye." The eye averages about 19 miles (30 km) in diameter, and the strongest winds occur in the "wall clouds" that surround it. Meteorologists use satellite pictures (see below) to track hurricanes, while aircraft and radar are used to collect data such as storm temperature, wind speed, and air pressure. Warnings can then be issued to people living in the hurricane's path. If possible, they will evacuate the area for the duration of the storm.

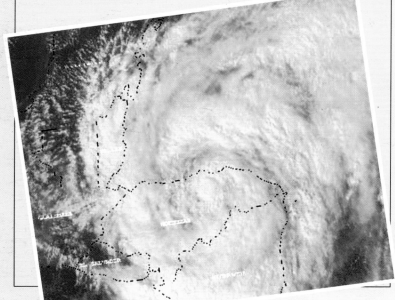

AS MANY AS TWO MILLION PEOPLE have been killed by hurricanes over the last 100 years. These ferocious tropical storms, which have a circular, whirling character, evolve out of areas of low air pressure that form over warm water regions of the Atlantic and eastern Pacific Oceans. (Similar storms occurring in the western Pacific Ocean are known as typhoons, and in the Indian Ocean as cyclones.)

Hurricanes bring with them winds of up to 186 miles per hour (300 kph), torrential rain, and prolonged thunder and lightning. The winds and rain, combined with the sea's force, produce huge waves called storm surges. These surges can demolish buildings and cause major flooding on a coastline. Some 90 percent of hurricane deaths are caused by flooding.

As a hurricane moves inland, it begins to lose strength. Still, rain and strong winds will continue to hit affected areas with destructive force for some time.

HURRICANE FACTS

- Hurricanes are given men's and women's first names in alphabetical sequence throughout the year.
- Wind speeds in a hurricane are measured in 5 levels of intensity:
  1 - 75-95 mph (weak)
  2 - 96-110 mph (moderate)
  3 - 111-130 mph (strong)
  4 - 130.5-155 mph (very strong)
  5 - over 155 mph (devastating)
- The diameter of a large hurricane can be as much as 404 mi., and the eye can measure up to 31 mi. across.

See also:
- **Hurricane Floyd, 1999: On the Rampage** *p. 36–37*
- **Tornadoes: Funnels of Fury** *p. 38–39*

Main areas of
hurricane activity

DISASTER AND DEVELOPMENT

The impact of hurricanes has varied according to factors such as the ability to track storms and the economic wealth of affected countries. In 1900, when there was little chance of predicting a hurricane, a storm surge on the coast of Texas killed more than 10,000 people. But the U.S. is a rich country—people

can afford to leave their homes—and U.S. meteorologists were soon able to give advance warning of storms. While the economic cost remains great (1992's Hurricane Andrew caused 22 billion dollars' worth of damage), the death toll has been reduced.

Another world
The story is very different in developing countries (such as Honduras, left). In 1963, a hurricane killed more than 5,000 people in Haiti, while there were more than one million storm victims in India and Bangladesh during the 1960s and early 1970s.

BELOW:
The aftermath of 1998's Hurricane Mitch, as survivors in one of the worst affected areas, Honduras, attempt to salvage something from the wreckage.

Spent winds
spiral outward.

Cool air
descends
in the "eye."

Thick buildup
of cumulus
clouds.

Hot air rises
rapidly.

Extremely strong winds
spiral into the
low-pressure center.

LEFT: *How a
hurricane forms.
The illustration clearly shows
the spiraling behavior of warm
and cold air over seawater.*

Hurricane Floyd, 1999: On the Rampage

FOCUS ON FLOYD

In the U.S., early warning systems have greatly reduced the numbers of people killed by hurricanes. The most effective method involves weather satellite observations (below, showing Floyd), which can spot the spiraling cloud bands at a very early stage.

But the story is quite different for people in developing countries such as El Salvador and Honduras. Even with adequate warning, many of those in the hurricane's path have neither the means nor the money to leave their homes.

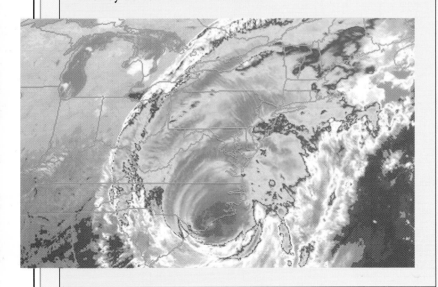

THE HURRICANE SEASON in the North Atlantic Ocean is between August and October, and the 1999 season produced one of the worst hurricanes in living memory. In September, Hurricane Floyd whirled over the Caribbean Sea, into the Gulf of Mexico, and then moved up the southeastern coast of the U.S. Major flooding affected more than 200,000 people in the states of North Carolina, New Jersey, and Virginia.

Yet the U.S. was far from being the worst hit country. When tropical storms left in the wake of the hurricane struck Honduras, the capital, Tegucigalpa, was engulfed by mudslides and countless numbers of people were made homeless. The situation was less severe in El Salvador and Costa Rica, but here, too, flooding rivers forced thousands to leave their homes.

ABOVE: *September 14—A satellite view of Hurricane Floyd as it spins at great speed past Florida up the southeastern coast of the U.S. Floyd was one of the largest of late-twentieth-century hurricanes.*

September 14: The storm an hour and a half after the main image (left).

September 15: Floyd wheels inland over the Carolinas and Virginia.

September 16: Its damage done, Floyd moves north and begins to break up.

RIGHT: *Air photograph of the eye of Hurricane Floyd.* BELOW: *Some of the devastation caused by Floyd. Though early warning systems in the U.S. have greatly reduced the number of hurricane deaths, rapid population increase in coastal areas might lead to greater disaster in the future if evacuation times are not sufficient.*

Tornadoes: Funnels of Fury

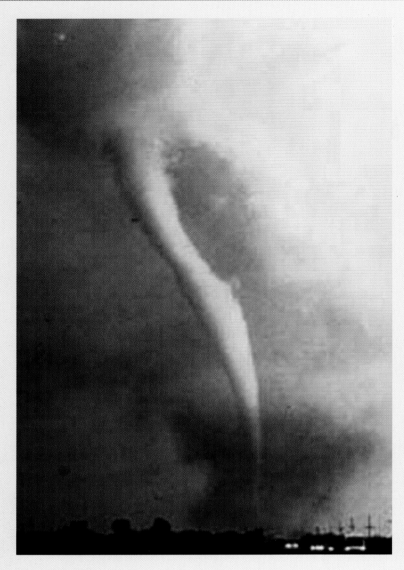

ABOVE: *Ideal conditions for tornado growth—towering cumulus wall clouds in a thunderstorm. The rounded masses at the bottom of the cloud have started to twist and form a funnel cloud extending to the ground.*

WATCHING AND WARNING

Tornadoes rarely last more than a few hours, and no two tornadoes are exactly alike. They are thus extremely difficult to predict, track, and study. Yet weather stations can issue a tornado warning when one has actually been sighted, or if a tornado-producing thunder-storm is indicated on a Doppler radar screen (right).

Low probability
Tornado watches and warnings save many lives. Moreover, it is very unlikely that any location will be hit by such storms more than once. In fact, a tornado is only likely to hit the same place in a tornado region about once every 250 years.

WITH A terrifying screeching noise similar to that of a low-flying jet, tornadoes whirl across the landscape at speeds of up to 62 miles per hour (100 kph) and wreak havoc wherever they go. Indeed, these spiral-shaped windstorms are responsible for more deaths each year than any other natural disaster except lightning and floods.

Tornadoes are created when cool, dry air collides with warm, moist air. Though they occur in many parts of the world, they are truly the scourge of the Midwestern and Gulf states of the U.S., where about 800 "twisters" are reported every year. Most do not cause much damage, but severe tornadoes are long remembered. On March 18, 1925, for example, a tornado whipped through over 186 miles (300 km) of the American Midwest. A total of 689 people were killed and well over 2,000 injured.

TORNADO TOLL

- The average annual death toll from tornadoes in the U.S. is 80 people.
- Between April 3 and 4, 1974, 148 tornadoes killed more than 300 people and injured 5,500 in 11 U.S. states.
- In 1931 in the U.S., a tornado carried a railway coach with 117 passengers 78 feet (24 m) through the air.
- The town of Codell, Kansas, was hit in three successive years by tornadoes—in 1916, 1917, and 1918—and each tornado struck on the same date, the 20th of May.

ABOVE: *Rotating air at the bottom of a storm cloud forms a narrow funnel cloud. If this reaches the ground, the weather system becomes a true tornado.*

See also:
- **Hurricanes: Storm Force** *p. 34–35*
- **The Dimmitt Tornado: A Texas Twister** *p. 40–41*

Main areas of tornado activity

FAR LEFT: *The scene of carnage after a tornado has roared its way through a rural community in the U.S. Even large, heavy vehicles (near left) are treated as mere playthings by the elemental force of these ferocious storms.*

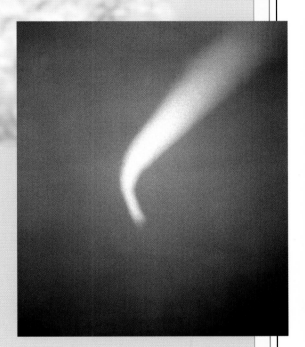

ABOVE: *The birth of a tornado in a violent thunderstorm. The rapidly rotating funnel—containing winds of up to 199 miles per hour (320 kph)—has not yet reached the ground, but the dust cloud shows that a "tornado touchdown" is imminent.*

Rising currents of warm, moist air form a rotating updraft.

Thundercloud develops into an anvil shape.

Cool, dry air flows downward.

As the cyclone of whirling winds increases in strength, the tornado is joined to the ground.

Debris is sucked up and blasted outward.

Path of tornado along the ground.

Main inflow of warm, moist air.

LEFT: *Anatomy of a tornado. The winds of a tornado rotate clockwise in the southern hemisphere and counterclockwise in the northern hemisphere.*

The Dimmitt Tornado: A Texas Twister

Dark wall clouds loom on the horizon near the town of Dimmitt.

A funnel cloud forms in midair—the beginning of the Dimmitt twister.

The funnel touches down and begins to whirl over the ground.

"Tornado Alley," which runs up the center of the U.S.

THE DAKOTAS
NEBRASKA
KANSAS
OKLAHOMA   ARKANSAS
TEXAS

DEATH ALLEY

A broad strip of land running the length of the U.S.— north from the Gulf of Mexico through the states of Texas, Arkansas, Oklahoma, Kansas, Nebraska, and the Dakotas to Canada— is popularly known as "Tornado Alley." In this area warm, moist air from the Gulf of Mexico frequently meets cold, dry air coming down from Canada. About 700 times each year, tornadoes are the result.

But freak conditions can con- found statistics. Between April 3 and 4, 1974, for example, 148 tornadoes ripped through 13 states. Some 315 people were killed. This violent 24 hours became known as the "1974 Super-Outbreak."

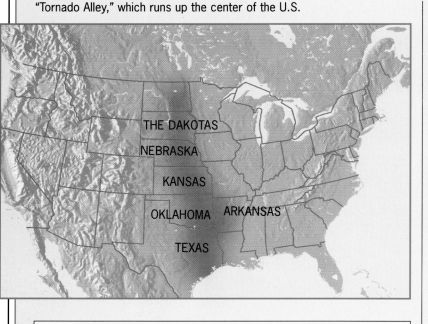

ON THE EVENING of Friday, June 2, 1995, a pow- erful tornado crossed Texas Highway 86 some 2 miles (3 km) from the small town of Dimmitt. It tore up 328 feet (100 m) of asphalt from the road and tossed it more than 656 feet (200 m) into a nearby field. Several cars were carried hundreds of feet (meters) and one house was destroyed. But within 10 minutes this twister had vanished.

Fortunately—and even though it was a strong, force 4 torna- do with a funnel one .62 miles (1 km) wide—the Dimmitt tornado caused no loss of life. Still, it was the most closely observed and completely monitored tornado in history, being followed across open fields from beginning to end by a group of meteorologists.

Using video cameras and chase vehicles specially equipped with meteorological instru- ments, the information these scientists gathered helped them to understand better than ever before how tornadoes form, develop, and function.

WIND FORCE

Tornado force can be measured accord- ing to the maximum speed of its winds:

Force	Wind Speed	Damage
F0	40 mph (65 kph)	Light
F1	75 mph (120 kph)	Moderate
F2	112 mph (180 kph)	Significant
F3	157 mph (252 kph)	Severe
F4	208 mph (335 kph)	Devastating
F5	262 mph (421 kph)	Incredible

Dimmitt rakes up the ground at the height of its power.

As its winds begin to abate, the tornado's hold on the ground lessens.

Dimmitt's funnel grows fainter and it fades into the distance.

ABOVE: *Tornado Dimmitt in mid-passage, the speed of its whirling winds reaching well over 208 miles per hour (335 kph).*

Lightning: Lethal Electricity

LIGHTNING AND THUNDER

There are many different forms of lightning. Forked lightning is seen as a bolt with many branches (see below, striking New York's Empire State Building), and streak lightning as a single jagged line. Ribbon lightning looks like parallel streaks of bright light, while chain lightning is a flash that forms a series of linklike streaks as it fades. Finally, ball lightning is literally a fireball that plummets to the ground.

Thunderclaps
The clap of thunder heard after the lightning is caused by the expansion of heated air. A deep rumbling is produced when lightning strikes some distance away, an earsplitting crash when the lightning is very near.

LIGHTNING KILLS more people in the Western world than any other natural force. In the U.S., for instance, twice as many people die from lightning strikes as fall victim to tornadoes. Most are killed as they take shelter under trees (natural conductors of electricity), or walk on golf courses, golf club in hand.

The most common type of lightning occurs within clouds, when a massive electrical spark is generated by the collision of positive and negative electrically charged particles. More dangerously, lightning can also be created by the collision of particles near the ground with those within a low storm cloud. Then lightning bolts can travel powerfully back and forth between the clouds and the ground.

ABOVE: *A deadly light show—multiple cloud-to-ground lightning strikes the Great Plains town of Norman, just south of Oklahoma City.*

SHOCKING FACTS

● Lightning strikes the Earth about 100 times every second worldwide.
● Lightning bolts discharge up to 100 million volts of electricity.
● St. Elmo's Fire, a glowing blue light around buildings and ships' masts, is caused by electrical discharges during storms.
● A lightning flash can consist of between one and 30 strokes, each stroke being fifty thousandths of a second apart.
● About 70 percent of fatal lightning bolts kill a single person, three-quarters of victims being men.

BELOW: *Forked lightning shooting from cloud to ground in the form of a "stepped leader"—so-called because of the step shapes of its separate bolts.*

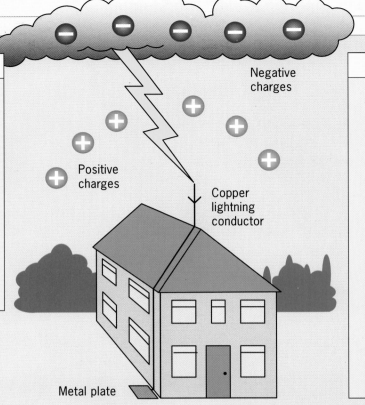

Negative charges

Positive charges

Copper lightning conductor

Metal plate

CONDUCTORS

A lightning conductor is usually a strip of copper on the side of a building that connects metal prongs on the roof to a metal plate in the ground. Positive electrical charges at the conductor's tip help to reduce negative charges in nearby thunderclouds, preventing the formation of lightning to some extent. But if lightning does form and proceeds to strike the house, it will hit the conductor first and the current will flow harmlessly down the strip into the ground.

Blizzards: The Blinding Snow

MISSILES FROM THE SKY

Large hailstones falling at a speed of 30 miles per hour (48 kph) can dent car roofs, and aircraft, smash windows, damage roofs and flatten crops. They can also kill human beings. Formed from freezing water in thunder- clouds, hailstones become bigger the longer they remain in the air. When they become too heavy for the air current to support, they fall to earth (see below). The biggest hailstone on record fell at Coffeyville in Kansas, in 1970. It weighed 1.65 pounds (0.75 kg) and was 6 inches (14 cm) in diameter.

BLIZZARDS ARE SNOW-STORMS swept along on fierce subzero winds, and are a particular menace in the U.S., Canada, and parts of northern Europe and Russia. Drastically reducing visibility and piling up large drifts of snow, they hamper all forms of transport and can strand motorists. People have frozen to death in their cars before rescuers had a chance to reach them.

Blizzards occur when cold air masses move down from northern Arctic zones into the warmer Temperate Zone. The cold air forces the warmer air to rise, and the rising air produces snow accompanied by cold northerly winds.

In an average blizzard, winds can reach speeds of 34 miles per hour (55 kph), visibility can fall to less than 492 feet (150 m) and temperatures plummet to as little as -54 °F (-12 °C). But in a severe blizzard, conditions may be much more extreme.

ABOVE: *A blizzard sweeps over a U.S. highway, making driving risky. Large vehicles with snow chains cope much better than the average car in such conditions.*

ABOVE: *An emergency pickup truck prepares to drag a stranded car out of a snowdrift. All forms of transport can be brought to a halt by blizzards, including aircraft (right).*

BELOW: *Snowplows attempt to clear the blizzard-hit streets of New York. Many U.S. cities are snowbound in winter—though no expense is spared to keep life as normal as possible.*

Drought: The Famine-Bringer

BLOWN BY THE WIND

Over large areas of the Sahel, overgrazing of cattle and deforestation have led to the creation of barren areas. Vicious sandstorms (below) then sweep away the topsoil and permanently degrade the land.

When their grazing land has turned to desert, farmers migrate to cities in the thousands. For example, Nouakchott, the capital of Mauritania on the west coast of Africa, had a population of 20,000 in 1960. Today the population is well over 350,000, over half of whom are refugees from drought.

IN CERTAIN PARTS of Africa, the Middle East, and the Indian subcontinent, it may not rain for months—even years—on end. The Sun beats mercilessly on the parched, thirsting soil, crops wither, and livestock perish. Starvation and disease inevitably follow for the human population. Worldwide, drought is responsible for about 20 percent of all deaths caused by natural disasters.

In many drought-prone areas of the world, rainfall is completely unpredictable. This may be due to a number of factors, including climate change, pollution, and the spread of deserts.

But whatever the reasons, few continents are as badly affected by drought as Africa. In one region alone, the Sahel, which lies south of the Sahara desert and extends across the center of the continent, untold numbers of people have died as a result of drought over the last 30 years.

ABOVE: *Cracked earth – grim evidence of long-term drought. This land may never recover, since the topsoil was blown away by the wind.*

See also:
- **Man-Made Deserts: Wastelands** p. 84–85
- **Messing with Nature: Disastrous Projects** p. 86–87

Areas of Africa most affected by drought

RIGHT: *Ethiopia, July 1989 – food distribution to refugees from drought-stricken Somalia. Emergency aid from Europe and Asia was airlifted to famine victims.*

LEFT: *A crowd of refugees awaiting food aid during one of the many Ethiopian famines of the 1980s. Over the last 30 years, droughts in Ethiopia, Somalia, Mali, and Mauritania have led to the mass migration of people from the countryside to cities (see below).*

Water: A Precious Resource

CREATING AND CONSERVING WATER

There are a number of ways of creating freshwater in drought areas. One is to remove salt from seawater—a process known as desalination. The desalination plants at Al Jubayl in Saudi Arabia, for example, produce 260 million gallons (1000 million L) of freshwater every day. But desalination is only effective near coasts, and is also very expensive. A cheaper way to produce water for crops is to cover them with clear plastic (below). Drops of condensation soon form on the inner surface of the plastic—a neat method of producing and conserving moisture.

THE AVERAGE HUMAN being needs to drink about 1.5 quarts (1 L) of water a day. Cattle need even more, and the pasture they feed on requires at least some rainfall in order to flourish. Crops, no matter how hardy, also need regular watering.

Though some of the world's poorest countries, such as Ethiopia, Mauritania, and Bangladesh, have been most severely affected by drought, richer countries have also suffered on occasion. Australia, for example, has had eight severe droughts since 1900, and in the U.S. in 1988 lack of rainfall in the Midwest caused a catastrophic crop failure.

But the story is not all one of disaster. People in drought-prone areas have sunk wells, developed irrigation schemes, and employed the latest technology to make parts of the desert green and fertile.

BELOW: *A flourishing desert farm in the United Arab Emirates. Unlike many African countries, the oil-rich Emirates can afford to use the latest irrigation technology to grow crops in the desert.*

WATER WONDERS

- In a person's lifetime, he or she will consume about 15,600 gallons (60,000 L) of water.
- Each person in a Western country uses about 68 gallons (260 L) of water in their home each day.
- Over three-quarters of the world's freshwater is frozen in the polar icecaps or in glaciers.
- Only about three percent of the Earth's water is fresh.
- The human body consists of about 65 percent water.

RIGHT: *A well on the outskirts of Khartoum, the capital of Sudan in northeastern Africa—a vital daily site for water-peddlers with barrels to fill and farmers with cattle.*

ABOVE: *An oasis in the Middle East. With their deep wells, canal systems, and sprinkler systems, such farms can produce a rich variety of crops all year round, including dates and citrus fruits. However, they are often expensive to maintain.*

THE ROOT OF THE PROBLEM

Improved farming methods and irrigation schemes are the only real solutions to drought in arid regions. In some parts of Africa, people cultivate gourds and roots that contain water (below), and put them in storage in case of hard times. Farmers can also move their livestock from one region to another to allow grazing land to recover.

Financing improvements
But money is needed to dig deep wells and construct irrigation systems. As a resource, this is perhaps even more scarce than water in certain African countries.

Wildfires: Forest Infernos

SURVIVAL OF THE FASTEST

Some trees such as the Australian eucalyptus and the redwoods of California can survive a forest fire, just as many grasses can survive grass fires. But unless animals flee (see below), or take shelter in underground burrows, their chances of survival are slim. Bushfires in Australia can move with incredible speed. In half an hour they can destroy as much as 1,000 acres (400 hectares) of forest – and most of the creatures that live there.

Threat of extinction
The equatorial rain forests are home to more species than any other habitat. But huge areas are put to the torch to clear land for farming, and it is thought that this brings about the extinction of more than 20 species every day.

A WALL OF CRACKLING flame advances through a forest, torching trees, scorching the earth, and forcing animals to flee for their lives. Meanwhile, firefighters equipped with power hoses desperately attempt to douse the blaze. . . .

Whether they are caused naturally by lightning or by a person throwing down a still-burning cigarette, forest fires can be immensely destructive. In the U.S. alone, they destroy up to 2 million (800,000 hectares) acres of forest land every year. And on one day in February 1983 in southern Australia, bushfires fanned by winds blowing at 50 miles per hour (80 kph) burned nearly 1 million acres (400,000 hectares) of land, killed more than 70 people, and left thousands homeless.

ABOVE: *A bushfire threatens a house in Australia. Such blazes are started almost every year during the dry Australian summer.*

See also:
- **Lightning: Lethal Electricity** *p. 42–43*
- **Summer Blazes: California Burning** *p. 52–53*

Regions prone
to forest fire

LEFT: *Firefighters clear a strip of land to create a firebreak ahead of oncoming flames. Vegetation is cut down and soil scraped away so that the fire has nothing to feed on.*

RISING FROM THE ASHES

From the earliest times, it was well-known that fire can actually improve the life of grasslands and forests by clearing them of choking vegetation and insect parasites such as wood-boring beetles. It was also common knowledge that the rich wood ash left by a fire helped new plants to grow stronger than ever before (right).

Slash and burn
So-called "slash-and-burn" cultivation, an ancient farming method, is still widely used in the forests and on the grasslands of South America, parts of Southeast Asia, and in Central Africa. Farmers cultivate an area of land for a year or two only, then move to a new area where they cut down the grass and trees and burn them. Ashes from the burned vegetation enrich the soil and make it fertile for crops for a short time – and then the process is repeated.

LEFT: *A firefighting plane dumps chemical "bombs" on a forest blaze. Aircraft are also used to observe fires, reporting on their size and direction.*

BELOW: *Fires in pine forests often have beneficial results.* **Left:** *Forest floor is covered with a blanket of rotting material.* **Center:** *Frequent fires pass quickly across the forest floor, ridding it of choking vegetation.* **Right:** *Only if the floor vegetation grows too high will the fire burn high and actually destroy trees.*

MAJOR FOREST FIRES

Date	Place	Area Destroyed
1871	Wisconsin, USA	1.7 million hectares
1983	South Australia	500,000 hectares
1988	Yellowstone Park, USA	610,000 hectares
1997-8	Indonesia	400,000 hectares

Summer Blazes: California Burning

ABOVE: *A woman surveys the charred wreckage of her home following the fires that swept through the suburbs of Los Angeles in 1972. Aircraft dropping chemical bombs (below) had only a minimal effect on the blaze.*

INHABITANTS OF SOUTHERN CALIFORNIA are constantly aware of fire hazards. In the Los Angeles and Santa Barbara areas particularly, long hot summers create tinder-dry conditions in the surrounding hills. A single spark is all that is needed to set the countryside ablaze.

In 1977, a fire reached to within one mile (2 km) of Santa Barbara's downtown area and burned 250 homes to the ground. In 1993, thousands of people in Los Angeles were evacuated as fires destroyed millions of dollars' worth of property along the southern California coast. And in 1994, a firestorm swept through the Los Angeles suburbs, melted the asphalt on the Pacific Coast Highway, and was halted only by the ocean.

ABOVE: *Beachfront houses in California threatened by approaching fires. Inland, only a swimming pool remained untouched by the fire that raced through a wealthy Los Angeles suburb (below).*

The External Threat: Space Debris

ABOUT 50,000 YEARS ago, a light of steadily increasing size appeared in the night sky. It was a 300,000-ton (16-km) meteor, and it entered the Earth's atmosphere above what is now Arizona. When the meteor crashed to the ground, it threw up a huge dust cloud and made a crater .75 miles (1.2 km) wide.

Scientists have found more than 120 meteor, comet, or asteroid craters on Earth. Though most "space debris" misses the Earth or burns up in the atmosphere, it can cause huge devastation when it collides with our planet. As recently as June 1908, for example, a comet hit Siberia with an explosion equivalent to that of a huge hydrogen bomb. Astronomers are even now scanning the skies for future threats from outer space.

ABOVE: *An artist's impression of the asteroid thought to have struck Central America 65 million years ago. Its impact affected the world's weather systems and may have brought about the death of the dinosaurs.*

DINOSAUR DOOMSDAY

Many theories have been put forward to explain the extinction of the dinosaurs about 65 million years ago. One suggestion is that an asteroid collided with the Earth. Heat from the impact threw billions of tons of dust into the atmosphere, blocking out the Sun. A catastrophic climate change followed, with temperatures well below freezing.

All plant life was destroyed, leading to the death of plant-eating dinosaurs and the carnivores that preyed on them. The asteroid that caused this catastrophe may have been responsible for the 112-mile-wide (180-km) impact crater found in Mexico (below).

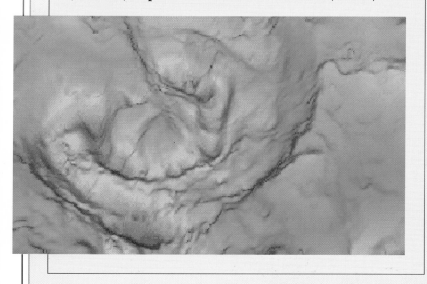

Right: *Comet Hale-Bopp above the Superstition Mountains in Arizona. With a solid nucleus of ice and a diameter of up to 10 miles (16 km), a comet can have a hugely destructive impact on a planet or moon.*

Below: *The bright streak of light in the night sky produced when a small meteor enters the Earth's atmosphere.*

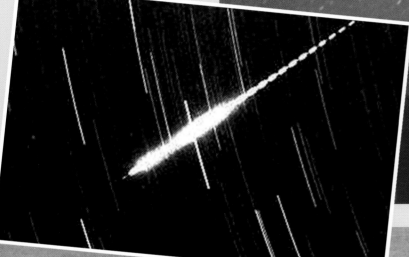

GREAT METEOR CRATERS

Location	Country	Diameter
Praha Basin	Czech Republic	199 mi (320 km)
Sudbury	Canada	124 mi (200 km)
Chicxulub	Mexico	109 mi (175 km)
Acraman	Australia	99 mi (160 km)
Vredefort	South Africa	87 mi (140 km)
Manicougan Crater	Canada	62 mi (100 km)
Duolun Crater	China	47 mi (75 km)
Kara Crater	Russia	31 mi (50 km)
Lake Huron Crater	Canada	30 mi (48 km)
Meteor Crater	U.S.	.75 mi (1.2 km)

Left: *574 feet (175 m) deep, the Meteor Crater in the Arizona desert is one of the smaller craters made on the Earth's surface by the impact of space debris.*

Troubled Waters

L IFE WOULD BE IMPOSSIBLE without water. Our bodies are two-thirds water, water covers over 70 percent of the Earth's surface, and over half the world's population lives within a short distance of rivers, lakes, and oceans.

Yet water can be a destructive element. Floods account for almost half of all deaths from natural disasters and devastate millions of acres of farmland every year. Tsunamis or giant sea waves have wreaked havoc on coastal communities throughout history. And coastlines are constantly being eroded or invaded by the sea, as the gradual warming of the Earth's atmosphere leads to rising sea levels and threatens the very existence of many low-lying countries.

Tsunamis: Waves of Terror

ABOVE: *April 1, 1946— a terrifying image of a man about to be engulfed by a tsunami over 299 feet (91 m) high breaking over the pier at Hilo, Hawaii.*

RIGHT: *Tsunami travel times for a quake occurring off the coast of Chile. Each curve represents two hours of travel time.*

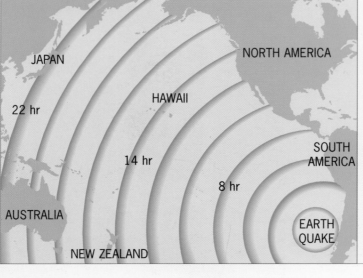

JAPAN

NORTH AMERICA

HAWAII

22 hr

14 hr

SOUTH AMERICA

8 hr

AUSTRALIA

EARTH QUAKE

NEW ZEALAND

THE SEABED is suddenly shaken by a series of violent tremors from an undersea quake. These tremors send vibrations upward through the ocean depths to the surface, and a low wave is formed. Though it probably cannot be felt by the ships it passes under, this tsunami (Japanese for "harbor wave") can travel at over 398 miles per hour (640 kph) and increases in size as it nears a coastline. Then a wall of water as tall as 89 feet (27 m) builds up—to crash on the shore and cause widespread death and destruction.

In 1896, more than 22,000 people were drowned when a 79-foot (24 m) tsunami struck Honshu, the main island of Japan. The wave originated from a quake 99 miles (160 km) out to sea, and passed harmlessly under the boats of local fishermen. Yet when they returned to shore, they found that their villages had all been swept away.

See also:
- **Earthquakes: The Shaking Crust** *p. 18–19*
- **Okushiri, 1993: A Tsunami Target** *p. 60–61*

Epicenter of seaquake on the ocean floor

Coastal shelf. The shallower the shelf, the greater the chance of tsunami buildup.

ABOVE: *Anatomy of a tsunami, showing the wave's buildup as it reaches a coast. Tsunamis often come in series—which can be fatal to anyone returning too soon to the scene of destruction.*

ABOVE: *The destruction caused to the island town of Kodiak, Alaska, by the Good Friday tsunami of 1964. The town of Seward, the mainland coast, also suffered greatly (below).*

TSUNAMI DISASTERS

Date	Place	Death Toll
1600 B.C.	Crete	Unknown
1755 (A.D.)	Lisbon	60,000
1868	Chile	25,674
1896	Japan	26,360
1933	Japan	3,000
1946	Alaska	200
1960	Chile	2,290
1976	Philippines	8,000
1998	Papua New Guinea	3,000

TSUNAMI ALERT

Whenever a seaquake occurs in the Pacific Ocean, its details are transmitted to Honolulu in the Hawaiian Islands from monitoring posts throughout the region. This information can provide the basis for a tsunami alert.

New technology

Still, such information can be unreliable. A total of 75 percent of all warnings issued since 1948 have been false. More recently, though, an efficient early warning system has been developed (see below). Pressure recorders on the Pacific seabed transmit information to buoys on the ocean surface. Transmitters on the buoys then send data to satellites, which in turn relay it to onshore bases.

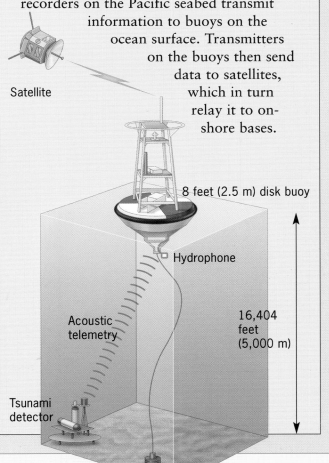

Satellite

8 feet (2.5 m) disk buoy

Hydrophone

Acoustic telemetry

16,404 feet (5,000 m)

Tsunami detector

Okushiri, 1993: A Tsunami Target

Complete devastastion at Aonae, caused by the tsunami and subsequent fires.

A clock lying in the debris at Aonae records the exact moment of tsunami impact.

Buildings reduced to matchwood at Aonae.

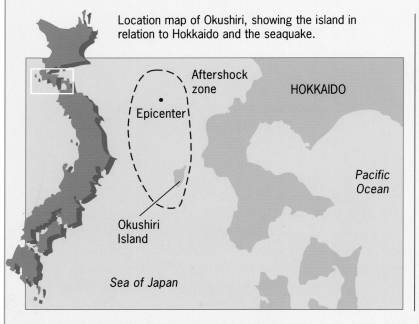

Location map of Okushiri, showing the island in relation to Hokkaido and the seaquake.

Aftershock zone

HOKKAIDO

Epicenter

Pacific Ocean

Okushiri Island

Sea of Japan

OKUSHIRI IS A SMALL ISLAND off the coast of Hokkaido, Japan. On the evening of July 12, 1993, a huge earthquake rocked Hokkaido's entire west coast. A major tsunami was set in motion, and 13 minutes later great waves up to 98 feet (30 m) high crashed onto the coasts of both Hokkaido and Okushiri.

Several towns along the Hokkaido coastline were badly damaged, but Aonae, a small tourist town on the southern tip of Okushiri, was simply devastated. Tragically, about 200 people lost their lives. But given the suddenness of the tsunami, it is a miracle this casualty figure was not higher.

In the days following the disaster, Japanese government survey teams visited 28 sites in the area, studying watermarks on buildings, lines of debris, and the wildlife and vegetation killed by salt water. They also found grim confirmation of the exact moment when the tsunami struck. Clocks flooded by seawater had all stopped at the same time—10:30 P.M.

LEFT: *Aftermath of the tsunami—a fishing boat thrown up onto the harborside at Aonae, Okushiri. Along with Hawaii and some islands of the South Pacific, Japan is particularly prone to tsunamis.*

A 15-foot (4.5 m) watermark on the side of damaged houses.

A fishing boat lifted up like a toy on to a concrete breakwater.

Seaweed swept inland by the tsunami hangs from an embankment.

LEFT AND BELOW: *Uprooted vegetation festoons telephone wires near Aonae. An aerial view of the south of Aonae in the aftermath of the disaster (below). This area was simply flattened by the great wave.*

Floods: Watery Havoc

HOLDING BACK THE WATERS

Flood warnings can save many lives, but they cannot prevent extensive damage when a flood strikes. To hold back rising floodwaters, people build levees or raised banks (see below) alongside rivers. They also dredge riverbeds to remove any piled-up silt that might raise the water level. Along coasts, stone and concrete seawalls stop flooding at high tide, as do dykes and hurricane barriers. Placing sandbags along the shores of seas, rivers, and lakes can also help to keep floodwaters at bay.

FLOODS ACCOUNT FOR over 40 percent of all natural disaster deaths worldwide. This is hardly surprising, perhaps, when one considers that more than half the world's population lives near large bodies of water.

Most rivers burst their banks about once every two years. But heavy rain or melting snow or ice can add 10 times as much water to normal river levels, causing large-scale floods on the surrounding plain. Lakes often overflow, too, while hurricanes may drive seawater inland in the form of tidal waves or storm surges. Collapsing dams can also imperil people in nearby valleys.

Floods can wreak havoc on a simply staggering scale. In 1938 in eastern China, for example, the Huang Ho River burst its banks. Nearly four million people perished, and it was many years before the land itself recovered.

BELOW: *Helpless before the power of the Ohio River, the streets of Shepherdsville, Kentucky, lie underwater following the floods of 1997.*

RIGHT: *Satellite pictures taken on July 2 and 17, 1993 showing the full extent of flooding in the upper Mississippi River basin. These floods caused major destruction to farmland.*

MISSISSIPPI MISCHIEF

A river meandering across a floodplain, like the Mississippi through the southern U.S., can bring both wealth and danger to the people living nearby. During a flood, the overflow of water deposits silt along the banks, which form raised barriers called levees. At the same time, silt is deposited on the riverbed, raising the water level (see below).

Bursting their banks

But after many floods, the river level rises above that of the surrounding countryside, the water being held back only by the levees. If heavy rain raises the level still farther, the levees may be breached. The Mississippi has burst its banks many times in this way.

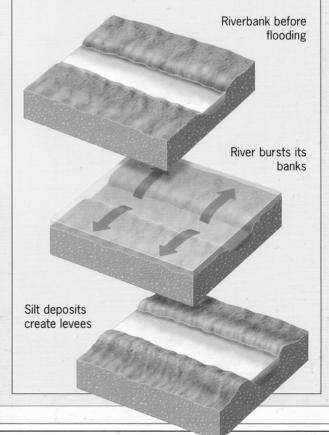

Riverbank before flooding

River bursts its banks

Silt deposits create levees

MAJOR FLOODS			
Date	Country	River	Deaths
1887	China	Huang He	1 million
1927	U.S.	Mississippi	500
1931	China	Yangtze	1 million
1938	China	Huang He	4 million
1991	Bangladesh	(sea floods)	150,000
1991	China	Yangtze	2,000
1991	Afghanistan	(flash floods)	5,000

ABOVE: *Citizens of Wertheim in central Germany resort to buckets and pumps after the nearby River Main burst its banks and flooded the streets.*

BELOW: *Bangladeshis wade along the watery streets of their capital, Dhaka. Floods often leave over half their country underwater.*

Honduras, 1998: A Deadly Deluge

Citizens of the capital, Tegucigalpa, watch helplessly as their city is engulfed by water.

Hondurans stranded by the collapse of a bridge in a muddy torrent.

People flee their homes, carrying whatever belongings they can.

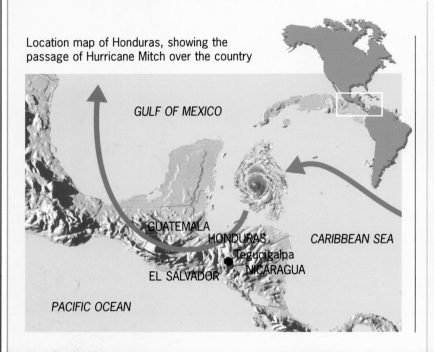

Location map of Honduras, showing the passage of Hurricane Mitch over the country

GULF OF MEXICO

GUATEMALA

HONDURAS

CARIBBEAN SEA

Tegucigalpa

EL SALVADOR

NICARAGUA

PACIFIC OCEAN

IN LATE OCTOBER 1998, Hurricane Mitch became the Atlantic Basin's fourth most powerful hurricane in history, bringing winds of up to 174 miles per hour (280 kph). When the storm hit Central America, it caused great damage to Guatemala, El Salvador, and Nicaragua. But nowhere was the devastation as severe as in Honduras.

From late on October 27 until the evening of October 29, Mitch hovered off the coast of northern Honduras. Then it moved inland—to dump over 25 inches (62 cm) of rain over the entire country in a 24-hour period. Soil on the hills came loose and formed mudslides that buried or swept away entire towns and villages. Rivers swelled to several times their natural size and the floodwaters rose to the second and third floors of offices and hospitals.

Over 10,000 people died in this catastrophe, two million were made homeless, and some 50 percent of the country's crops were destroyed. It will take Honduras many years to recover.

LEFT: *October 30, 1998—cars and trucks are abandoned as surging floodwaters from the Choluteca River fill the streets of Tegucigalpa, the capital of Honduras.*

One of the many bridges destroyed by the rapidly rising waters.

One of the few farm animals to be saved—a chicken is carried above the floodwaters.

A fireman desperately searches flooded wreckage for survivors.

LEFT AND BELOW: *The eye of the storm. This dramatic air photograph captures the eye of Hurricane Mitch and a satellite view of the storm brewing.*

LEFT: *Children are drafted in to dig out mud-swamped houses in the aftermath of Hurricane Mitch. Over 100,000 homes and other buildings were destroyed in Honduras as a result of the floods. Many low-lying rural areas were simply drowned (below).*

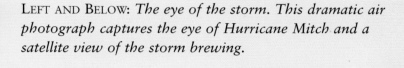

Coasts in Peril: The Rising Sea

PROTECTING LONDON

Sea levels are rising in the North Sea. One day, high tides and storm surges might cause a tidal wave to sweep up the Thames estuary and engulf London, the capital of the Great Britain.

To prevent such a disaster, in 1982 a flood barrier was built across the Thames at Woolwich (below). When a very high tide is due, the gates are raised to stop the tidal water flowing upstream. Still, if sea levels continue to rise at their present pace, by the middle of the twenty-first century even this barrier may not provide London with sufficient protection.

MILLIONS OF PEOPLE live on or near sea coasts, which stretch for many thousands of miles around the world. Yet while for most there is little to fear from the sea, some could be in great danger.

ABOVE: *Waves shatter over the seawall of an English coastal town. High seas in winter are responsible for much coastal erosion.*

The land is slowly sinking and the warming up of the Earth's atmosphere is causing the oceans to expand. Over the past 100 years, the world's sea level has risen by between 5 and 10 inches (10–25 cm), and by the end of the twenty-first century it may rise by more than 20 inches (50 cm). If the atmosphere continues to get warmer, the polar icecaps will gradually melt, causing the sea level to rise even more.

In this event, many of the world's great coastal cities would suffer disastrous flooding. Low-lying countries such as Bangladesh would be virtually destroyed, and island nations such as the Maldives in the Indian Ocean would simply disappear beneath the waves.

See also:
- **Hurricanes: Storm Force** *p. 34–35*
- **Tsunamis: Waves of Terror** *p. 58–59*

MIGRANT ISLANDS

Islands make up the total landmass of some countries, such as the United Kingdom, Japan, and the Philippines. Many islands were formed hundreds of millions of years ago, but new ones are still being created. The volcanic island of Surtsey, for example, rose from the sea off the coast of Iceland as recently as 1963.

Once an island is created, the sea will constantly change its shape, eroding solid matter from one place (see below) and transferring it somewhere else. Waves batter shorelines, tides ebb and flow, and over time islands can actually "move" in the oceans.

ABOVE: *Bangladeshi men piling up sandbags on the storm-battered coast of their country, which is prone to sea flooding. Concrete blocks (right) also help to prevent coastal erosion.*

BELOW: *A composite image showing some typical features of coastal erosion. The way a coast is eroded by the sea may depend on various factors such as tides, currents, and rock types.*

Natural arches are formed when wave action wears away relatively soft rock.

Headlands are formed by relatively wave-resistant, hard rock.

Groynes slow down the erosion of beaches. Both straight and zigzag groynes perform much the same function of hindering the drift of sand along the shore.

A stack is a pillar of rock left isolated by the erosion of a headland.

A tombolo – a piece of land still connected to the mainland by piled-up sand.

A spit, or baymouth bar, which forms when sand and pebbles pile up in the entrance of an inlet.

El Niño: Current of Change

Normal flow of trade winds breaks down

Equatorial countercurrent

Reversed flow
of mid-Pacific
currents during
El Niño

Humboldt current

ABOVE: *A satellite image of La Niña ("girl child"). Unlike El Niño, La Niña is cold water topping an unusually low sea level in the central Pacific (see purple patch). But by deflecting winds, it also changes world weather patterns.*

EL NIÑO (meaning "boy child" in Spanish) is a warm ocean current in the central Pacific Ocean and part of the global circulation of waters that affect weather conditions in many parts of the world.

ABOVE: *The normal flow of ocean currents is reversed during an El Niño year. Normally the strong currents flow westward. When El Niño occurs, there is eastward movement along the South American coast.*

Occurring once every three to seven years, El Niño varies greatly in its effects according to its warmth. In 1982 and 1983, for example, the warmest El Niño on record caused weather extremes worldwide. Severe drought struck Australia, Indonesia, and the Philippines, causing huge crop failures and loss of life. Meanwhile, fierce storms struck the California coast and heavy snows in the Sierra Nevada and the mountains of Utah and Colorado led to flooding and mudslides.

During other El Niño years, warm areas of water off the coast of Ecuador and Peru blocked the welling up of the colder, nutrient-filled water, and fish stocks were severely affected.

See also:
- **Floods: Watery Havoc** *p. 62–63*
- **Coasts in Peril: The Rising Sea** *p. 66–67*

ABOVE: *The coast near Pacifica, California, is hit by storms caused by El Niño in 1998. After the storms died down, extensive erosion became evident (below). Many people were evacuated before the sea could claim their houses.*

BELOW: *An aerial photograph taken at high tide at Cape Blanco in Oregon, U.S., before El Niño of 1997–98. The same spot photographed at high tide in January 1998 (below right) shows the extent to which the sea's behavior has changed.*

THE DISENCHANTED ISLES?

Once known as the "Enchanted Islands," the Galápagos are a series of volcanic peaks in the Pacific Ocean west of Ecuador. Many unique animals live there, including marine iguanas (below) and giant tortoises.

Threat to wildlife

But the Gálapagos lie directly in the path of El Niño. In recent years the current has caused disastrous droughts on the islands, and killed off large areas of algae on the rocky coast. Many iguanas perished, since the aquatic plant is their staple diet.

The Human Impact

HUMAN BEINGS HAVE ALWAYS had to endure natural disasters such as earthquakes, storms, droughts, and wildfires. In the last 200 years or so, however, humanity itself has begun to have a disastrous effect on the planet's environment.

The atmosphere is being polluted by fuel exhausts, burn-off from power stations, and smoke from waste sites. The oceans are being contaminated by oil spills from supertankers and chemical dumping. And the destruction of our tropical rain forests is threatening both the atmosphere and the survival of hundreds of thousands of animal species.

Stemming the tide of environmental pollution will depend not only on government action, but on industry and—above all—the actions and attitudes of ordinary people across the world.

Air Pollution: Choking the Planet

ABOVE: *Smog over Mexico City, one of the most polluted cities on Earth. Mexico City also contains some of the world's poorest shanty towns, and poverty makes the fight against pollution even more difficult.*

ABOVE: *Traffic fumes rise from the streets of Manila, the capital of the Philippines. Containing harmful gases such as carbon monoxide and hydrogen sulphide, such fumes force many people to wear face masks (right).*

A THICK HAZE shrouds busy city streets, industrial chimneys belch out smoke, and burning garbage releases harmful gases into the air. These are just a few forms of atmospheric pollution—a problem that now threatens the very future of our planet.

Every day, poisonous gases and tiny particles of liquid or solid matter are released into the atmosphere. Most of this pollution stems from the burning of petrol, coal, gas, and oil to run motor vehicles and power stations. The two main culprits are smog and acid rain. Smog is a brownish haze that develops when released gases react with sunlight, while acid rain is rain poisoned by acids given off by the burning of fossil fuels. Both cause great harm to the environment and to living creatures.

See also:
- **Volcanoes: The Fire-breathers** *p. 12–13*
- **Smog: The Hazardous Haze** *p. 74–75*

NATURAL POLLUTANTS

Some air pollutants are produced naturally, and may then combine with pollution caused by humans. Examples are:

- Ash clouds from volcanoes
- Ozone from breaking seas
- Smoke from forest fires
- Pollens and essential oils from plants
- Bacteria and viruses
- Dust clouds

ABOVE: *An environmental group makes a dramatic protest against carbon dioxide emissions.*

BELOW: *Smoke pours from the chimneys of a coal power station in Germany.*

THE OZONE HOLE

The ozone layer is a form of oxygen in the upper atmosphere that shields the Earth from up to 99 percent of the Sun's harsh ultraviolet rays. Without its protection, life on the planet would probably die out.

But now air pollutants are putting the ozone layer at risk. Chemicals called CFCs, used as coolants in refrigerators and air-conditioning plants and for producing foam insulation, are leaking into the atmosphere and thinning the ozone layer—particularly over the Antarctic during the southern hemisphere spring.

A hole in the Earth's atmosphere

This "ozone hole" (see above, shown as blue in the satellite photo) covers an area more than twice the size of the U.S. Despite action taken by governments to cut down on the use of CFCs, those chemicals still in the atmosphere will continue to affect the ozone layer for at least another 50 years. The ozone hole will need constant monitoring by scientists living in such bases as the British Antarctic Survey Station (below).

Smog: The Hazardous Haze

THE LAST BREATH

Many of the world's major cities suffer from smog. A satellite view of Santiago, the capital of Chile, reveals how air pollution can spread over a large area (below, highlighted in red). Other smog-prone modern cities include Mexico City and Athens, the capital of Greece.

Bad as the air can be in these places, smog once had a more instantly lethal effect. In 1952, 4,700 people died of breathing-related diseases within five days when a "pea-souper" lay over London.

EVERY DAY THE AVERAGE PERSON inhales about 26,000 gallons (10,000 L) of air. During an average lifetime, that adds up to enough air to fill a football stadium. If this air were polluted, then the risks to health are obvious.

Smog is a particular health risk in many cities. A brown mixture of ozone and particulates (liquid or solid matter) that develops from the emission of car exhaust fumes, smog can cause headaches, breathing problems, and eye irritation. Over time, it may even be the cause of more serious diseases.

In the city of Los Angeles, the fumes from over five million cars on the often jammed freeway system create a smog that has its worst effects 19 to 37 miles (30 to 60 km) downwind. The city authorities have been trying to combat this problem for some years, improving public transport and discouraging dependence on cars.

BELOW: *A smog-blurred view of Los Angeles and a Californian landscape. Such pollution can be at its most severe when it combines with intense heat or humid air.*

ABOVE: *The hills surrounding Los Angeles are hazed over by smog on a hot summer's day. Smog has a destructive effect on plant life as well as on humans.*

BELOW: *Columns of traffic on the freeway entering Los Angeles. Emissions from cars, trucks, and other forms of transport account for nearly half the air pollution in the U.S.— which produces more air pollution than any other single country.*

Sea Pollution: Oceans at Risk

Overfishing is a serious menace to the world's fish stocks. As the Earth's population has grown, so has the demand for fish and shellfish, which are full of protein. Most industrial nations now have fleets of huge factory ships (see below) with electronic detection devices for hunting fish, and over 90 million tons of fish are taken from the seas annually. If these stocks are not replaced, and the amount of fish caught controlled by law, then much of the world's supply of fish could disappear—along with a fishing industry that employs millions of people worldwide.

T HE OCEANS COVER more than 70 percent of the Earth's surface, and in some places are 36,089 feet (11,000 m) deep. Without the oceans to supply water for rainfall and to regulate the temperature of the atmosphere, the Earth would be a lifeless desert.

Yet despite their great size, the world's oceans are threatened by pollution. Harmful waste products including crude oil, industrial chemicals, and sewage or human waste are being dumped into the sea in ever greater quantities.

Billions of tons of plastics are also dumped into the sea annually. These include materials thrown overboard from fishing boats, container ships, and other vessels. Since these plastics do not break down easily, they continue to pose a major threat to fish and other marine creatures.

RIGHT: *Since 1989, oyster populations in the Chesapeake Bay area— once notable for this delicacy—have been steadily reduced by an unidentified agent. Possibly a rise in water temperature or a virus was responsible.*

RIGHT: *At the end of the 1980s, about 10,000 acres (4,000 hectares) of turtle grass, which provides a home to many fish species, were killed in Florida Bay by an unknown agent. Another 57,500 acres (23,000 hectares) were also affected.*

RIGHT: *In the 1980s, Caribbean sea urchins, important herbivores in the marine food chain, were virtually wiped out by a mysterious infection. This also had a disastrous effect on the region's coral reefs.*

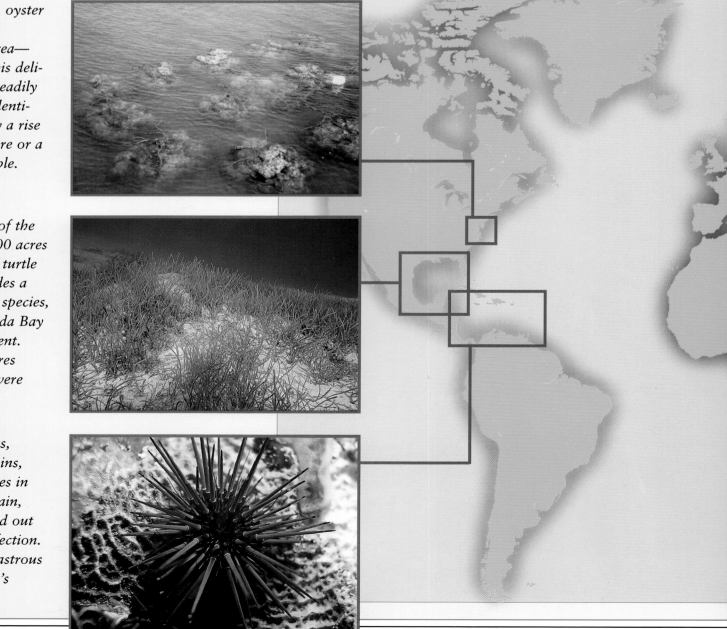

See also:
• **Air Pollution: Choking the Planet** *p. 72–73*
• **Black Seas: Oil Pollution** *p. 78–79*

RIGHT: *Sewage pumped into the sea contains bacteria that use up the water's precious, life-giving oxygen. By killing off plankton and thus the larger creatures that feed on them, bacteria can effectively turn areas of ocean into "dead zones."*

BELOW: *According to scientists, pollution, sea farming, and an increase in viruses due to global warming are causing disastrous outbreaks of disease among marine life. Unless these problems are tackled, extinction could follow for many species.*

LEFT: *The unique freshwater seals of Siberia's Lake Baikal —the largest body of freshwater in the world—have become infected with a distemper virus caught from domestic dogs.*

LEFT: *Coral reefs in the Indian Ocean are suffering the worst epidemic of "bleaching" (coral death) in recorded history. The death of algae that live on the coral is thought to be chiefly responsible.*

LEFT: *Bluefin tuna off the coast of South Australia have suffered from a large-scale virus epidemic. An infection from frozen feed in nearby fish farms was the cause.*

Black Seas: Oil Pollution

THE GULF DISASTER

The world's largest oil spill took place during the Gulf War of 1991, when Iraq deliberately released half a billion gallons (1.75 billion L) of oil into the waters of the Persian Gulf. The oil slick (below, highlighted in red) threatened to contaminate one of the world's largest desalination plants in Saudi Arabia, and extended for over 37 miles (60 km) around the Saudi Arabian island of Abu Ali. The resulting pollution did immense long-term harm to the Gulf's wildlife and ecosystem.

MODERN SUPERTANKERS are monstrously large, and can carry as much as a million barrels of oil. If a supertanker breaks up in a storm or runs aground, millions of gallons (liters) of this poisonous black cargo can pour into the sea. Such spills, or slicks, from tankers or oil wells often kill large numbers of fish, seabirds, and other marine animals, and may ruin the environment for years to come.

Although some supertankers have double hulls to cut down on oil loss, accidents persist, and billions of gallons (liters) of oil are spilled into the sea every year. In 1989, for example, the supertanker *Exxon Valdez* ran aground in Prince William Sound, Alaska, and disgorged 12,944,820 gallons (49 million L) of crude oil. Hundreds of miles (km) of unspoiled coast were polluted and thousands of animals— seals, seabirds, whales, and fish—perished.

BELOW: *An aerial photograph of an oil skimmer working to clean up a 1990 oil spill in Galveston Bay off the coast of Texas.*

ABOVE AND RIGHT: *Horrifying scenes from the aftermath of the 1996* Sea Empress *oil slick, which washed ashore at Milford Haven on the west coast of Wales. The slick ruined beaches and killed thousands of seabirds.*

LEFT: *The* Exxon Valdez *in Prince William Sound, Alaska. Another tanker is in the process of taking on the remainder of the stricken ship's oil.*

MAJOR OIL SPILLS

Date	Location	Amount of Spill
1978	Coast of France	67 million gallons (257 million L)
1979	Gulf of Mexico	127,400 million gallons (490 million L)
1989	Alaska	13 million gallons (49 million L)
1991	Persian Gulf	.5 billion gallons (1.75 billion L)

CLEANING UP AFTERWARD

Supertanker and oil well accidents in the oceans account for only a small proportion of ocean pollution. When they do occur, however, something must be done immediately if the long-term effects are not to be disastrous. One method of cleaning up a slick at sea is to place a ring of buoyant pumping and skimming devices around it to collect the oil. Another is to place sheets of oil-absorbent material on the ocean surface, and yet a third is to burn the oil —though this can cause considerable air pollution. Lastly, detergents can be used. But these, too, can kill fish and damage the marine ecosystem.

Coastal catastrophe
Oil spills on a coastline can have a catastrophic effect on local wildlife. Despite attempts to break up the oil using power hoses (right), birds that have already been covered in oil are often poisoned when they attempt to clean their feathers. Efforts by people to clean birds (left) usually save only a fraction of the affected population.

Deforestation: A Chainsaw Catastrophe

ABOVE: *Parts of the Amazon rain forest being cleared by fire, as seen from a satellite. The destruction of the rain forests is harmful to the Earth's atmosphere, leading to global warming.*

GUARDIANS OF THE SOIL

Forest fires are often deliberately started by people in order to clear the land for farming. In recent years, this has occurred extensively in Indonesia (below)—with disastrous consequences for the land itself. Since trees absorb large amounts of rainwater, they prevent the rapid runoff that causes soil erosion and flooding on a massive scale. The proof of the value of trees is that the soil on many Indonesian farms established on former forest land has been all but washed away.

DAY AFTER DAY in parts of the Amazon rain forest, the buzzing whine of chainsaws, the splintering crack of wood and the crash of foliage announce that yet another giant tree has been felled. For, like the great rain forests of Asia and Africa, the Amazon is shrinking. In fact, of the 4 million square miles (10 million square km) of the world's surface covered by rain forests, about 60,000 square miles (150,000 square km) are being cut down every year. Greed for timber and farmland are the chief reasons for such wanton destruction.

Yet forests are vital to the world's well-being. Not only do they provide us with timber and food such as fruits and nuts, as well as with drugs and with substances such as resin and rubber, they help to preserve the balance of gases in the Earth's atmosphere by absorbing carbon dioxide and releasing oxygen. Forests also help to conserve soil and water and are home to millions of living creatures. The devastation must be halted or reduced soon if the world is not to face natural disaster on an unprecedented scale.

ABOVE: *Amerindians in Venezuela clear small areas of forest in a sustainable fashion for crop-planting. But in Brazil, huge swaths of forest are cut down for highly prized hardwood timbers such as mahogany (right).*

BELOW AND RIGHT: *Trees killed off by acid rain in northern Europe. Acid rain strips away a tree's leaves and bark, leaving it to die a slow death.*

BELOW: *A map showing the major sites of deforestation. Logging and clearance pose the chief threats to the equatorial rain forests, pollution to the temperate northern forests.*

AMAZING TREES

● The baobab tree of Africa can have a trunk 49 feet (15 m) in diameter and can live for over 1,000 years.
● Californian redwoods 361 feet (110 m) tall have been recorded.
● Tropical rain forests have more tree species than any other forest—179 types can be found in just 2.5 acres (1 hectare).
● The upas tree's sap once provided poison for the arrows and darts of local tribesmen. It grows in Southeast Asia and was supposed to bring death to any bird that perched on it.
● A giant sequoia in California is the world's largest living thing. It is nearly 276 feet (84 m) tall, its trunk is 36 feet (11 m) wide, and it is at least 2,000 years old.

ABOVE: *Forest fires rage on the Indonesian island of Sumatra. Such fires are started illegally to clear land for farming. Although forest products are major Indonesian exports, their exploitation is unsustainable at the present rate.*

LEFT: *Trees felled in the African country of Cameroon. The bark is stripped for sale to pharmaceutical companies for drug manufacture. By contrast, in some parts of Indonesia edible pod-producing petai trees are being planted by local people on destroyed forest land (right).*

Importing Pests: The Australian Story

FOREIGN GLUTTONS

The cane toad (below) is the Australian name for the giant marine toad of Central and South America. Known for its voracious appetite, in 1935 it was imported to the sugarcane fields of Queensland to eat the beetles and grubs that threatened the crop. But the cane toad's introduction was a catastrophe for other local species: It also has a taste for fish, other amphibians, birds, and even small mammals. It bred tremendously quickly and soon became a serious pest in many parts of Australia.

DESTRUCTION OF NATURAL HABITATS and overhunting are two of the ways in which humans bring about the extinction of animal and plant species. But living things can also be endangered by the introduction of alien species. Nowhere was this seen more vividly than in nineteenth- and twentieth-century Australia, when a host of imported animals displaced native species and became pests.

Rabbits, for example, had no natural enemies in Australia. With plenty of grassland to feed on, the rabbit population rapidly soared to over 500 million, overrunning the grazing land of sheep and taking over the burrows of native marsupial species such as the bandicoot. The Australian grasslands were also invaded by rats and mice brought in by European ships. When cats were brought in to deal with them, they, too, ran wild, and proceeded to decimate the populations of native birds.

BELOW: *A camel in the outback. Camels were introduced as pack animals because they could easily cope with Australia's deserts. Today, large numbers run wild, threatening grazing land.*

ABOVE: *The prickly pear cactus, which was introduced to Australia in 1788 to be used in dye production. The cactus spread so fast that by 1925 it covered 30 million acres (12 million hectares) of farmland. Today, most prickly pears have been cleared from the land.*

See also:
- **Drought: The Famine-Bringer** *p. 46–47*
- **Man-Made Deserts: Wastelands** *p. 84–85*

LEFT: *A pair of dingoes, the wild dogs of Australia and one of the continent's top beasts of prey. Introduced to Australia from Asia by Aborigines 7,000 years ago, the dingo's rise in numbers probably caused the extinction of the native marsupial wolf. Its favorite prey is the wallaby, but it has also been known to kill sheep.*

RIGHT: *The European rabbit—innocent-looking but hugely destructive in large numbers. Attempts to control it culminated in the deliberate introduction of the disease myxomatosis in the early 1950s (its effects can be clearly seen in this photograph). Though 99 percent of rabbits were destroyed at the time, their numbers have since recovered.*

ABOVE: *A herd of water buffalo, which were introduced by settlers to Australia's Northern Territory. More than 200,000 now run wild there, consuming enormous amounts of food and water. They are now hunted for their hides and meat.*

Man-Made Deserts: Wastelands

GREAT DESERTS

Sahara – 3,440.000 sq mi. (8,600,000 sq km)

Arabian – 932,000 sq mi. (2,330,000 sq km)

Gobi – 520,000 sq mi. (1,300,000 sq km)

Great Victoria – 258,000 sq mi. (647,000 sq km)

Kalahari – 200,000 sq mi. (500,000 sq km)

SPREADING THE SAHARA

The Sahara in North Africa covers a surface area greater than that of the U.S. But it was not always the vast sea of sand it is now. At Tassili-n-Ajjer in Algeria, rock paintings some 7,000 years old (below) depict cattle, water-loving hippopotamuses, and people apparently taking their ease in lush surroundings. And Roman ruins also prove that much of this area was fertile just 1,000 years ago. One of the causes of its later desertification was probably greed for timber.

SHIPS STRANDED in the middle of a desert and camels stalking over what was once one of the world's biggest bodies of inland water…. Such sights might seem to belong to science fiction, but they are common in the central Asian state of Uzbekistan—and are startling evidence of the death of the Aral Sea.

Since 1960, when irrigation schemes diverted the two main rivers that fed its waters, the surface area of the Aral Sea has shrunk by more than 50 percent. As a result, the once flourishing fishing industry has been destroyed and the 35 million people of the region impoverished. This is just one dramatic way in which human activity can lay waste the environment. But overgrazing by cattle, destruction of trees, poor farming methods, mining, and soil erosion also all contribute to the spread of barren land or deserts.

See also:
- **Deforestation: A Chainsaw Catastrophe** *p. 80–81*
- **Messing with Nature: Disastrous Projects** *p. 86–87*

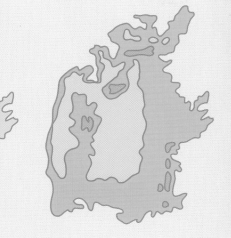

LEFT: *Camels now replace ships as a means of transport in the Aral Sea. Since 1960, the Aral Sea has lost over 70 percent of its water (above). The remaining salty grit is blown by winds as far as the Arctic Ocean and nothing can live on it.*

ABOVE: *Tractors trundle over dry fields in Washington State, stirring up great clouds of dust from the land. Over-intensive land use can lead to soil erosion—and the eventual creation of barren land.*

LEFT: *Bad irrigation schemes such as those in Uzbekistan can create deserts as fast as they counter them. But better controlled schemes can offer the inhabitants a greener future.*

MAKING THE DESERT BLOOM

Whether deserts are natural or man-made, people in arid regions are thinking of ways to stop their spread and are trying to reclaim barren land. The most ancient and successful method is irrigation, which was used by the Egyptians over 5,000 years ago when water was diverted from the Nile River to their fields via an elaborate canal system.

Modern oases

Today, in many desert areas of the southwestern U.S., Egypt, and Libya (see right), farming would be impossible without water brought by irrigation. Many dams have been built to create reservoirs for irrigation water—though sometimes dam construction can cause as many problems as it solves. Less harmfully, in Israel's Negev Desert farmers collect dew to water their fields.

Messing with Nature: Disastrous Projects

THE CHERNOBYL CRISIS

More sustainable than fossil fuels, nuclear power was once thought of as a solution to many of people's energy needs. The drawback lay in the highly poisonous nature of nuclear fuel, uranium.

In 1986, an explosion in a nuclear power plant in Chernobyl, in the former Soviet Union (below), sent radioactive clouds drifting as far as central Europe. At the site itself, at least 30 people died from burns and many more were exposed to radiation, which causes cancer.

MODERN SCIENCE HAS SOLVED many of the ills and problems of mankind. Cures have been found for once incurable diseases and living conditions have improved for millions of people. Life expectancy has increased—or at least in the developed world.

Yet the uncontrolled, thoughtless, or deliberately destructive use of technology has brought with it a host of new problems. Accidents have taken place at nuclear power stations, and shortsighted irrigation schemes have drained whole regions of their precious water supplies. Poisonous chemicals have been released into the atmosphere or the sea, and dams built that have had unforeseen consequences on the surrounding landscape.

Only with long-term planning and the best scientific advice may such environmental disasters be averted in the future.

BELOW: *Testing a nuclear bomb. Nuclear tests in Australia and the South Pacific have left large areas of radiation-poisoned land that may take centuries to become fully safe.*

See also:
- **Air Pollution: Choking the Planet** p. 72–73
- **Sea Pollution: Oceans at Risk** p. 76–77

ABOVE: *Iraq's deliberate destruction of Kuwait's oil wells during the Gulf War of 1991, which led to massive air pollution in the region.*

DAMAGING DAMS

There are over 100 superdams more than 492 feet (150 m) high worldwide. While many of these have brought significant benefits to nearby populations, providing water for irrigation and electric power, others have caused unforeseen problems. For example, it is thought that the Hoover Dam (below) in

the U.S. caused a series of earthquakes in the 1930s: Water had seeped into old faults in the Earth's crust and widened them.

The Aswan High Dam in Egypt (above) has also affected the natural environment, causing the erosion of the Egyptian coastline, depriving the Nile delta of flood silt that enriches the soil, and spawning a plague of parasitic worms that spread the disease bilharzia.

Overpopulation: People Pressure

ABOVE: *The skyscrapers of Manhattan tower over New York, one of the world's largest cities. With a total population of 15 million, New York City suffers from urban sprawl—the gradual spread of a city into outlying districts. Throughout the world, there are more than 2,000 cities with a population of over 100,000 and about 225 with over one million.*

IN THE 200 YEARS between 1650 and 1850, the world's population doubled. But from 1850 to the 1990s, with the huge advances in modern medicine, it increased by nearly five times. The figure in the year 2000 stands at over six billion. If population growth continues at its present rate, by 2050 there may be as many as 9.3 billion people on Earth.

Overpopulation exerts many pressures on the natural environment. Of the world's entire population, over 500 million people live in overcrowded cities—and these cities are swallowing up more and more land. The planet's remaining wildernesses are under threat, pollution is on the increase, and the demand for precious natural resources is soaring. Unless population growth is cut, there may also be a greater chance of worldwide famine and epidemics.

BELOW: *A location map of some of the world's major cities, highlighting the environmental problems they face.*

Athens, Greece: Athens' air pollution is the worst in western Europe. During some summers, individual cars are only allowed in the city center every other day.

Shanghai, China: Four million tons of untreated waste are discharged daily into the Huangpu River. This often produces a black, foul-smelling gas.

Toronto, Canada: A fire outside the city in a dump of 14 million tires could be seen for 80 miles (130 km) in early 1990. People were evacuated and vast amounts of oil seeped into the water table.

São Paulo, Brazil: The waste products of heavy industry in this city lead to acid rain with a pH below 4.5—over 1,000 times more acidic than normal water.

Cairo, Egypt: The largest city in northern Africa, Cairo treats less than half its sewage. The rest finds its way into the Nile and the lakes. Contagious diseases are common.

Bombay, India: At least three and a half million people live in slums, and 40 percent of housing has open sewers.

See also:
- **Deforestation: A Chainsaw Catastrophe** *p. 80–81*
- **Man-Made Deserts: Wastelands** *p. 84–85*

OUT OF CONTROL?

There have been many schemes to control the birth rate and achieve "zero population growth" (two children per family), where only enough people are born to replace those who die. Focusing on a mixture of education and fertility reduction, such schemes have had limited success: Families in the poorest countries still have an average of eight children.

RIGHT: *People swarm through the streets of Dhaka, the capital of Bangladesh. With a population of over six million, this city suffers from increasing traffic congestion and pollution.*

GETTING AWAY

With the world's population concentrating in cities, people are becoming more and more cut off from the natural environment. In the relatively prosperous West, this has led to a trend for adventure or ecotourism—holidays in the world's remaining untouched wildernesses, such as Antarctica (below). While such trips may increase general knowledge about the wild and its importance, they exert pressures of their own on fragile environments.

MEGACITIES

The world has over 20 megacities—urban centers with populations of more than 10 million:

Tokyo-Yokohama, Japan	29,500,000
Mexico City, Mexico	26,000,000
São Paulo, Brazil	24,000,000
Seoul, South Korea	21,000,000
New York City, U.S.	15,000,000
Bombay, India	15,000,000
Osaka-Kobe-Kyoto, Japan	14,000,000
Calcutta, India	13,500,000
Rio de Janeiro, Brazil	13,500,000
Teheran, Iran	13,000,000

ABOVE: *Rio de Janeiro's shanties hug the hillsides round the city and provide homes for thousands of poor people. Such conditions are a breeding ground for disease.*

Disasters and History

I F THE EARTH'S AGE is thought of as a year, the whole course of human history would amount to far less than a fraction of a second. But during that time, the destinies of entire peoples have been closely bound up with the planet's natural history.

The Great Famine

A vivid illustration of how natural disaster can change human history is provided by the Irish potato famine of the mid-nineteenth century. When the country's crop was devastated by a fungus, poor people began to starve. More than 750,000 died, and many more emigrated. For a long time, Ireland remained a relatively depopulated country.

A Disastrous Future?

Elsewhere, too, epidemics, climatic change, and the spread of deserts have all had an impact on history. The ultimate disaster will be the expansion of the Sun, which in about three and a half billion years will be so hot that life on Earth will die out. But in the interim, it is certain that more Earth-based catastrophes will continue to shape our world.

ABOVE: *A.D. 79—Pompeii during the eruption of Vesuvius.*

The End of Pompeii

In A.D. 79, the volcano Vesuvius in southern Italy erupted, sending lava and hot ash pouring down onto the thriving Roman towns of Pompeii and Herculaneum. Buried to a height of 10 feet (3 m), the life of the two towns came to an abrupt end, and the eruption was so sudden and catastrophic that many of the inhabitants were overtaken by the flow of lava. The hollows left by some of their bodies were excavated in the twentieth century, and plaster casts made from them reveal the victims' agonizing last moments.

A Quake in Human Thought

The earthquake and tsunamis that hit Lisbon, the capital of Portugal, in 1755 killed more than 60,000 people. But apart from the terrible toll taken on human life, this disaster had other, far-reaching effects on human thought. At this time a number of leading European philosophers were questioning the role of God

ABOVE: *1755—Lisbon lies in ruins following the great quake.*

ABOVE: *1902—St. Pierre following the eruption of Mt. Pelée.*

in human affairs. Among them was the Frenchman Voltaire, who wrote a highly influential poem questioning the "mercy" of a Christian God who could let so many men, women, and children perish in a single catastrophe.

Krakatoa Reborn
A still more devastating tsunami was generated in 1883 by the explosion of the volcanic island of Krakatoa, in what is now Indonesia. Though the wave passed unremarked through some of the world's busiest shipping lanes, when it struck the shores of Java and Sumatra it

ABOVE: *1883—Krakatoa begins to erupt.*

killed about 36,000 people. The story, however, would not appear to end there. In 1952, following a series of undersea explosions, a new cone rose from the depths of the Java Sea—evidence that volcanic activity in the area may again be severe.

A Capital Catastrophe
But the most terrible volcanic disaster in history took place in 1902 on the small

Caribbean island of Martinique. Mont Pelée, a volcano towering over the capital at the time, St. Pierre, erupted and sent an incandescent cloud of ash rolling down its slopes. Almost everyone in the town was killed—about 30,000 people. The only survivors were a prisoner in a deep prison cell and a shoe-

maker who had hidden beneath his work-bench. The capital of Martinique is now Fort-de-France.

Preparing for the Future
Japan is one of the most earthquake-prone countries in the world: Thirteen major quakes hit the island chain between A.D. 684 and 1946.

The most devastating quake of all struck the city of Tokyo in 1923, when more than 99,000 people were killed. Since then, the city's authorities have introduced measures that may reduce the casualty rate of any future disaster. Every year on the anniversary of the 1923 quake, the first of September, the whole population undergoes intensive escape and rescue drills.

ABOVE: *1923—the aftermath of the great Tokyo earthquake.*

Glossary

A

Algae
Seaweed or related plants that grow in water.

Amerindian
Native peoples of South America, many of whom have their homes in the rain forest.

Asteroid
A large rocky object orbiting the Sun, thought to be material left over from the formation of the solar system.

Atmosphere
The layer of gas surrounding the Earth.

Axis
The angle at which a planet's north pole points in relation to its orbit. For example, the Earth's axis is tilted 23° relative to its orbit of the Sun.

B

Bacteria
Microscopic organisms found in countless numbers in air, soil, living bodies, and decomposing matter. Some types can cause disease.

Birthrate
A measurement of population growth: the number of births in one year for every 1,000 persons.

C

Climate
The mean or average temperature and rainfall that a large area of land has over a long period.

Comet
A small icy object surrounded by gas and dust that moves in a highly elliptical orbit around the Sun. Comets that pass near the Sun leave bright "tails" of gas and dust.

Conductor
In physical terms, any material or object that transmits electricity or heat.

Crater
A circular hollow or depression in the surface of a planet or moon, usually the result of meteor impact.

Crude oil
The raw material from which petroleum is made.

Crust
The surface of the Earth.

Cyclone
The term for a major tropical storm in the Indian Ocean.

D

Debris
Fragments of objects such as houses and machinery that may be destroyed in a flood, landslide, or other disaster. The term can also refer to pieces of rock thrown up by a volcanic eruption.

Deforestation
The general term for the removal of forests from a landscape.

Desalination
The process by which salt is removed from seawater and made suitable for drinking.

Detergent
A substance such as soap or other synthetic product that is used to clean soiled objects.

Developing country
One of the poorer nations of the world, which still has few resources and little industry.

Dike
A barrier made of earth or other material built to prevent a river from overflowing its banks or to stop the sea from flooding the land.

E

El Niño
A warm current in the Pacific Ocean that often affects weather systems worldwide.

Emissions
Gases given out into the atmosphere. Vehicle exhaust fumes and industrial smoke are examples.

Environment
The surrounding conditions of a place, especially as they influence the development and growth of living things.

Epicenter
The point on the Earth's surface directly above the underground origin or source of an earthquake.

Equator
The imaginary line running around the center of the Earth or other planet.

Erosion
The process by which rocks and soil are loosened and broken up by the action of air or water.

F

Fault
In geophysical terms, the line in the Earth's crust where two tectonic plates meet.

Firebreak
A strip of land cleared by firefighters to deny a forest fire fuel.

Floodplain
Low-lying land on either side of a river that can be flooded periodically.

Focus
The point underground where an earthquake begins.

Fossil fuels
Fuels such as oil and coal, which are produced over thousands of years by decaying vegetable and animal matter and are found underground.

G

Global warming
The gradual warming of the Earth's atmosphere because of gases given off by industry and transport.

Gravity
The fundamental property of matter, which produces the mutual attraction of objects.

Greenhouse effect
The warming of the Earth's surface produced when the atmosphere traps the heat of the Sun.

Groin
A wall or fence, often of wooden stakes, built across a beach to prevent erosion.

H

Habitat
The place where an animal or plant lives.

Hardwood timbers
Highly valued wood from rain forest trees such as teak and mahogany.

Hemisphere
Half of a sphere such as a planet or moon.

L

Latitude
A coordinate for determining positions on Earth or other planet north or south of the equator.

Lava flow
The name given both to the movement of lava down a volcano's slopes and to the lava in its hardened state.

Levee
Raised banks along a river created by the deposit of silt, and sometimes built up to prevent further floods.

M

Magnitude
In geophysical terms, the measure of the strength of an earthquake.

Mantle
The matter surrounding the core of the Earth.

Mass
The measure of a body's resistance to acceleration.

Meteor
A relatively small rocky object left over from the formation of the solar system. Thousands of meteors orbit the Sun and some enter the Earth's atmosphere.

Meteorologists
Scientists who study, record, and analyze the weather.

O

Oil slick
A mass of oil floating on or just under the sea's surface.

Orbit
The line of motion of one object in space as it moves around another.

Oxygen
Gas in the atmosphere that makes up one-fifth of the volume of air and is vital to all living things.

Ozone
A form of oxygen in the Earth's upper atmosphere.

P

Pesticide
A group of chemicals used to kill pests such as insects, weeds, and rats.

Planet
A large body in space that orbits a star.

Pollutant
Any substance that damages the natural environment and can harm the health of living things.

Pyroclastic flow
A fast-moving mass of lava and volcanic ash that can cause widespread damage.

Q

Quagmire
Thick mud formed by heavy rain or floods.

R

Radioactivity
The release of energy as the result of atomic activity. Some radioactive substances, such as some forms of uranium, occur naturally.

Rain forest
An area of dense evergreen trees and other vegetation situated near the equator and home to a great variety of living creatures.

Richter scale
Measurement of the magnitude of an earthquake, as it is registered on a seismometer. A quake measuring six on the scale is 10 times stronger than one measuring five.

The American geophysicist C. F. Richter compiled the scale in 1935, basing his readings on seismometers located 62 miles (100 km) from the epicenters of various quakes. The highest magnitude any earthquake had registered before the year 2000 was 8.6.

S

Satellite
Objects that orbit other objects in space—normally applied to spacecraft orbiting the Earth.

Seaquake
An earthquake originating on the seabed.

Seismic
From the Greek "seismos," meaning earthquake. Anything that has to do with earthquake activity.

Seismometer
An instrument that measures and records ground movements and can determine the position and strength of an earthquake.

Sewage
Waste matter from homes and factories that is usually carried away in sewers or drains for dumping or for conversion into nontoxic substances.

Smog
A form of air pollution mainly caused by exhaust gases from motor vehicles.

Species
Classification of living things that have common characteristics but are different from others in at least one way. Members of the same species can breed with each other.

Storm surge
The above-normal rising of the sea along a coast as a result of strong winds.

T

Tectonic plates
The 30 or more moveable sections that form the Earth's crust.

Tiltmeter
An instrument used for measuring the expansion of a volcano, and thus the swelling of magma inside it.

Tsunami
From the Japanese, meaning "harbor wave"—a large and often highly destructive wave or series of waves produced by a seaquake.

Typhoon
The name given in the western Pacific Ocean to a hurricane.

V

Vent
In reference to volcanoes, the opening in the Earth's crust through which magma and gases seek escape.

W

Wall cloud
A kind of thundercloud that can produce a tornado.

Index

Acknowledgments

The publishers wish to thank the following organizations and individuals for providing photographs for use in this publication

l=left, *r*=right, *t*=top, *c*=center, *b*=bottom

6 *tr*, *bl* USGS; 7 *tr*, *bl* NOAA; 8 *tl* Planet Earth Pictures, *br* NIFC; 9 *tl* EOSAT, *br* John Isaac/Still Pictures; 10 *c* NOAA, *inset* USGS; 11 *bl*, *br* Corbis; 12 *tl*, *bl* NOAA; 13 *tl*, *cr*, *b* NOAA; 14 *t* USGS/R McGimsey, *bl* USGS/B Chouet; 15 *tl* USGS/M E Yount, *bl* USGS/M Mangan, *br* USGS/K McGee, *cr* USGS/J D Griggs; 16–17 *(tx6)*, *bl*, *c* USGS; 17 *cr*, *b* USGS; 18 *bl* NOAA; 19 *b* NOAA; 20 *cr* US National Archives/Heritage Picture Library, *bl* NOAA; 21 *t*, *b* NOAA; 22 *t*, *inset*, *bl* USGS; 23 *tr*, *b* USGS; 24 *bl* Tony Stone Images; 24–25 *b* Corbis; 25 *inset* Corbis, *tr* Tony Stone Images, *tl* Corbis; 26–27 *(tx6)* Corbis; 26 *cl*, *bl* Corbis; 27 *b* Corbis; 28 *t*, *b* Corbis; 29 *cl*, *cr*, *b*, Corbis; 30 *bl*, *br* Corbis; 30–31 *br* Corbis, *c* Popperfoto; 31 *cr* Popperfoto, *br* J Allan Cash; 32 *c* NOAA, *inset* Gerard & Margi Moss/Still Pictures; 33 *bl*, *br* NOAA; 34 *t* Gerard & Margi Moss/Still Pictures, *b* NASA; 35 *cr*, *cl* Nigel Dickinson/Still Pictures; 36 *t*, *b* NOAA; 37 *(tx3)* NOAA, *b*, *inset* Corbis; 38 *tl*, *bl*, *cr* NOAA; 39 *tl*, *tc* Popperfoto/Reuters, *cr* NOAA; 40–41 *(tx6)* NOAA; 40 *b* NOAA; 41 *b* NOAA; 42 *t*, *b* NOAA; 43 *b* NOAA; 44 *t* Corbis, *b* USGS; 45 *tl*, *tr* Corbis, *b* Rex Features; 46 *t* Planet Earth Pictures, *b* Tony Crocetta/Still Pictures; 47 *tl* UNHCR, *c* Heine Pedersen/Still Pictures, *b* Heine Pedersen/Still Pictures; 48 *t* Paul Harrison/Still Pictures, *b* Romano Cagnoni/Still Pictures; 49 *cl* Romano Cagnoni/Still Pictures, *tr* Carlos Guarita/Still Pictures, *br* Ron Giling/Still Pictures; 50 *t* NIFC, *b* Tantyo Bangun/Still Pictures; 51 *tl*, *cl* NIFC, *cr* Planet Earth Pictures; 52 *t, b*, Rex Features; 53 *t*, *b* Rex Features; 54 *bl* USGS; 54–55 *b* NASA; 55 *tr*, *inset* USGS; 56 *c* Rex Features, *inset* NOAA; 57 *bl* Peter Frischmuth/Still Pictures, *br* Shehzad Noorani/Still Pictures; 58–59 *t* NOAA; 58 *cl* NOAA; 59 *tr*, *bl* NOAA; 60 *(tx6)* NOAA, *b* NOAA; 61 *inset*, *b* NOAA; 62 *tl* Thomas Raupach/Still Pictures, *b* Planet Earth Pictures; 63 *(tx2)* USGS, *cl* Peter Frischmuth/Still Pictures, *bl* Shehzad Noorani/Still pictures; 64–65 *(tx6)* Corbis; 64 *b* Corbis; 65 *cl*, *b* Corbis; 66 *t* Rex Features, *b* Mark Edwards/Still Pictures; 67 *tr* Shehzad Noorani/Still Pictures, *cr* Gil Moti/Still Pictures, *cl* Planet Earth Pictures; 68 *bl* NOAA; 69 *tl*, *cl*, *bl*, *br* USGS, *cr* Rex Features; 70 *c* Mike Schroders/Still Pictures, *inset* Dylan Garcia/Still Pictures; 71 *bl* Mark Edwards/Still Pictures, *br* Voltchev-UNEP/Still Pictures, *t* Julio Etchart/Still Pictures; 72 *cl* Julio Etchart/Still Pictures, *b* Tantyo Bangun/Still Pictures; 73 *tl* Sabina Vielmo/Still Pictures, *bl* Klaus Andrews/Still Pictures, *tr* NOAA, *br* Planet Earth Pictures; 74 *tl*, *b* USGS; 75 *t*, *b* USGS; 76 *tl* Mark Edwards/Still Pictures, *tcl* NOAA, *bcl*, *b* Planet Earth Pictures; 77 *t* Dylan Garcia/Still Pictures, *tcr*, *br* Planet Earth Pictures, *bcr* Norbert Wu/Still Pictures; 78 *tl* EOSAT, *b* Jim Olive/Still Pictures; 79 *tl*, *tr* Paul Glendell/Still Pictures, *c* Al Grillo/Still Pictures, *bl* Still Pictures, *br* Al Grillo/Still Pictures; 80 *t* NASA/Still Pictures, *bl*, *cr*, *br* Mark Edwards/Still Pictures; 81 *tl* Hartmut Schwarzbach/Still Pictures, *tr* Andre Mascennikov/Still Pictures, *cr* Tantyo Bangun/Still Pictures, *bl*, *br* Mark Edwards/Still Pictures; 82 *tl* Tony Stone Images, *bl*, *br* Corbis; 83 *t* Planet Earth Pictures, *cr*, *b* Corbis; 84 *t* Gil Moti/Still Pictures, *b* D Escartin/Still Pictures; 85 *tr* A Maclean-Peter Arnold Inc/Still Pictures, *cl* Peter Stemerding/Still Pictures, *b* Vultchev-UNEP/Still Pictures; 86 *t* Rex Features, *b* US Government/Los Alamos; 87 *t* Pierre Gleizes/Still Pictures, *bl* Planet Earth Pictures, *br* Jurgen Schytte/Still Pictures; 88 *t* Mike Schroders/Still Pictures; 89 *t* John Isaac/Still Pictures, *cl* John Maier/Still Pictures, *br* Mark Edwards/Still Pictures; 90–91 *all* Heritage Picture Library